Preface

I was born in 1964 in Huddersfield and raised in Northumberland, and since I was a child I've been creating my own businesses. In 1992, with a £50,000 investment, I co-founded HomeServe, a home repairs and improvements company. It quickly became a FTSE-250 listed business, serving over 8.5 million customers worldwide, and is set fair to become the global market leader in residential infrastructure. HomeServe was sold for £4.1 billion in 2023 to the Canadian private equity giant Brookfield Asset Management.

Now I devote my time to inspiring breakthroughs in other entrepreneurs and CEOs at an earlier stage in their journey. In 2023, I succeeded James Timpson and Martha Lane Fox as the *Sunday Times* business columnist, and I use that column to focus on the problems business leaders face as they tackle their growing pains and opportunities. Around the same time, I bought a magazine called *Business Leader*, and this, alongside a sister podcast and newsletter, has evolved into a community of entrepreneurs and CEOs who inspire each other to accelerate their growth. We're helping some of the 75,000 medium-sized businesses in the UK to become large companies. If we can double the number of large businesses in the UK to over 15,000, then we can make a significant difference to the health of the UK economy.

Through Growth Partner, my investment business, I've also used £100 million of my own money to back thirteen entrepreneurs, and I've committed to invest another £100 million in a further thirteen over the next three years. Meanwhile, my charity, The Enterprise Trust, funds programmes to inspire young people to start their own businesses.

I'd like to think my approach to business is grounded and uncomplicated; I certainly hope it's humane. Here, in your hands, are nine business lessons I wish I'd known when I started, and which I hope will fit a new generation of leaders for a world of extraordinary challenges, and a market exhausted by business as usual.

Whatever success I've achieved, I put it down almost entirely to the leaders I have recruited; as a breed, they're far more talented than me. The list is a long one, and even then, it feels painfully incomplete. Among them are Jennifer Synnott, Jonathan King, Rachael Hughes, Guillaume Huser, Stephen Phillips, Tom Rusin, John Kitzie, Fernando Prieto, Ross Clemmow, Edward Fitzmaurice, Greg Jackson, Craig Wright, Ian Carlisle, Martin Bennett, David Bower, Jonathan Ford, Mike Jackson, Nick Kasmir, Thomas Rebel, Gerard Downes, Jason Mahendran, Jambu Palaniappan and Shaun Prime.

You'll hear from some of these people in this book. I'll also narrate some of my more spectacular scrapes and mistakes, sharing the lows as well as the highs of my breakneck entrepreneurial career. In meetings I tell people, 'Listen to what I say; don't just do what I do.' I'll leave it to you to judge what I did, what I should have done – and what I should have left well alone.

Introduction

A family story has it that, when I was six years old, our school class had to write an essay about their pets. Mine read: 'I have twelve rabbits, Flopsy, Mopsy, Topsy . . . Flopsy is worth 2p; Mopsy is worth 4p; Topsy has just had 12 babies, each of which can be sold for 1p . . .' So, is this a quirky story about a boy who fell in love early with business? Or is it a minatory tale about an imbalanced personality?

Well, you decide. If you want answers to some of business's most intractable problems, this book is for you. If you want easy answers, though, you might want to look elsewhere. Achievement comes at a price, and this book is about the price, as well as the prize.

Should you take my advice? I think you should. But I don't expect you to take my advice uncritically. You need to know who I am. You need to do your due diligence.

You should know that, as a boy, I built businesses the way my school friends built Airfix kits. By the age of seven I had pivoted my rabbit-breeding business into a kennels service (much more profitable). I ran the school tuck shop from my locker at the Royal Grammar School in Newcastle. Come conker season, I hired my mates to shake conkers (horse chestnuts) from the trees (more efficient than throwing sticks at them), and sold them, carefully graded, in plastic bags to a network of school-age distributors.

I developed a certain flair. At nine years old, I appeared on the stage of the Grand Hotel in Harrogate in front of five hundred members of the Northern Magic Circle. Though not a natural raconteur (I still get a touch of nerves when speaking in public), I quickly learned, from my all-too-brief career as a stage magician, that business has plenty of show business in it.

One wheeze I started at school, tying together fishing flies for anglers, grew big enough that when I sold up, straight after university, it paid for a car and the 10 per cent deposit on my first house, in Gosforth in Newcastle, a five-minute drive to work at the consumer goods giant Procter & Gamble. And while I was training there in marketing, I very nearly lost my shirt selling Christmas trees in pub car parks.

For me, business is a vocation, like painting, or singing, or building the Taj Mahal out of matchsticks. Business is not rocket science. It is neither an intellectual game nor a private members' club. Success in business awaits those who let the art of business consume them, heart, mind and soul.

For those inspired to action, *How to Make a Billion in Nine Steps* will help you identify your passions and core abilities, and encourage you to ruthlessly eliminate distractions and diversions in your pursuit of your best self and your best business. I want to share the joy and worth, as well as the effectiveness, of entrepreneurial thinking.

Will you make a billion? Different business sectors offer different levels of reward, and it may be that in your chosen sector, no amount of outstanding success will allow you to reach that magic number. But that's fine, and it's no excuse for you not to think big.

Set a target appropriate for you, but make it a big one. Set yourself a challenge serious enough that it scares you. For example, in the UK, there are only 7,500 large companies – that is, companies who employ more than 250 people – and yet these companies employ 40 per cent of the UK workforce. Imagine the good you'd be doing if only your business earned a place among this elite group!

In any event, aiming for the stars is the only way you'll ever reach the moon.

It's not enough for me to tell you how I made a business worth billions. I need to give you a feel for the process, so that you can make your own decisions, and build your own best business.

In Chapter One, 'Copy and Pivot', I'll show how my two best-known businesses, HomeServe and Checkatrade, found success by solving real customer problems, rather than by chasing 'disruptive' buzz-words. We constantly learned from others – especially our competitors – and adapted proven ideas to create even better solutions.

Chapter Two, 'Find an investor', is about finding the right partners, at the right time, to support your vision and help you grow. Investors are partners, not cash machines, and we need to seek investors whose values align with ours. Trying to raise investment when you've run out of money is very bad timing, and I gave away far too much of my business early on.

Coaching and mentoring are the focus of Chapter Three. A successful businessman who initially rebuffed my approaches eventually offered invaluable guidance that helped HomeServe accelerate its overseas operations. I hope, reading this chapter, you'll be inspired to embrace the power of mentorship and coaching to gain strategic insight, clarity of focus and continuous learning.

Chapter Four, 'Bricks and clicks and paper', is about my career-long efforts to bind the real and virtual worlds into an effective 'omnichannel' business strategy. The internet is not going away, but it is getting cluttered, and it is becoming eye-wateringly expensive. As I write this, I can't help but notice a return to the values I embraced at the start of my career, to do with real-world market testing and careful measurement. I'll explain how traditional marketing methods can work smoothly to support a strong digital presence.

Time flies. No sooner do we get a handle on business than it seems we're letting go. Nonetheless, 'Be a smarter leader – hire your replacement'. In Chapter Five I argue that to truly focus on your business, you need a stellar team – people who outshine you and need the freedom to take your company to new heights.

My sixth secret is, 'Go global with locals', and it's possibly my hardest-won lesson. Throughout HomeServe's life, we've been trying to expand into new markets. We've succeeded (spectacularly, in some cases), but just as often it's been a bruising experience. It's been beaten into me to respect geography, and distance, and local knowledge. HomeServe's overseas expansion offers many lessons ('business has plenty to learn from show business' being not the least of them). I'll show how we've stayed true to our core, while embracing local expertise.

HomeServe grew by constantly adapting and innovating. We embraced a bias for action and we haven't been afraid to experiment or make mistakes. We regarded even the most serious setbacks as opportunities – even a government action that overnight robbed us of our key product. Chapter Seven, 'Evolution, not revolution', is about our need to constantly innovate, stay nimble and nurture an entrepreneurial mindset throughout our businesses.

Saying 'No' is hard, but I've learned it's the most powerful business move you can make. Chapter Eight, 'Follow a *not*-to-do list', is my moment to step into the confessional. Chasing every shiny new idea is, I have discovered, a recipe for distracted mediocrity. True success lies in focusing on your core strengths and ruthlessly eliminating distractions.

In 'Hone your character', the ninth and final chapter, we'll look back over what we've covered and I'll try to pick out those elements of personal character that suit us to be entrepreneurs. Some of us learn to be entrepreneurs (quite late in our career, in some cases). Others (and I'd have to count myself among them) seem born to the task. In the long run, though, it doesn't much matter which group you belong to: no one arrives perfectly able to do everything. For all of us, entrepreneurialism is a learning game. We should develop our strengths by learning, and mitigate our weaknesses by surrounding ourselves with the right people – I've certainly had to.

One of my favourite tactics, when I conduct interviews, is to ask the candidate to tell me about a significant achievement or adversity they experienced in childhood. I'm not being nosey. I'm looking to see what lessons they've derived from life. So here, in turn, is a bit of my story, and where these lessons began.

Where did I get my entrepreneurial streak? Family must have had a hand in it: my great-grandfather was a successful Yorkshire cloth merchant. The family's fortune was wiped out in the Great Depression of 1929, and its entrepreneurial zeal took a serious knock. As a young man, my father, David, nursed an interest in property and antiques, but even auctioneering was too radical-sounding a vocation for his parents, who urged him into a civil service career.

My great-grandmother on my mother's side helped to set up and run a thriving cotton mill in Huddersfield. The family shipped cotton waste from the mills to Kentish hop farmers, who used it as manure. The bottom fell out of that market just as they had invested in a fleet of lorries. Undaunted, my grandmother launched herself into a florist's business and ended up running a successful property business in Cleckheaton in Yorkshire.

But, for all this business heritage, it seems to me that two, seemingly unrelated, incidents in my childhood inspired my career. The first involved a helicopter: every month a chopper brought Lord Hanson, a famous corporate raider, rattling over our home in Birkby, Huddersfield. He'd land in the garden of his parents' bungalow, at the end of Stanwell Avenue, where we lived until I was four. What small boy could resist the lure of such a lifestyle, glimpsed over the garden wall?

My other driving memory is of my mother's vain efforts to give me a day out on a newly reopened narrow canal. The free boat rides had just ended by the time we arrived. Mum begged, close to tears, and kept getting the brush-off; Lord Hanson would never have been treated like that!

Years later, I am still driven by these memories, which are fundamentally about power and freedom to set your own course. Yes, I fly my own helicopter (though I'm as likely these days to take the environmental option and travel by train), but I reckon the business of stripping the assets of dying companies, as Hanson did, would bore me senseless. I prefer to stake my fortune on healthy businesses, bringing them to new levels of success. As for the social clout I once imagined Hanson-level success would bring – well, that's real enough, I suppose, but I've learned its limits. Not long ago I bankrolled the recovery of my local pub, only I keep forgetting that I still have to book a table at least three days in advance.

So there you have it. My life is about as strange – and about as ordinary – as everyone else's. Whatever it is that drives you – a dream or a nightmare, a good memory or a bad one – what matters is the lessons you draw from it. We all have some entrepreneurial potential, and while success in business is sometimes driven by a past experience, what happened is not the crucial element.

What matters is *the lesson you learned*. Here, in these pages, you'll find the nine lessons that I have drawn from my own success, and which I believe will inspire success in your own business.

Before you begin ...

This book is the result of three decades of building, learning, and scaling a £4 billion business. To help you apply what's inside, I've created a set of free tools and resources that build on the Nine Steps you're about to discover.

They're designed to help you accelerate your growth – and avoid the mistakes I made along the way.

To access them, visit businessleader.co.uk/bonus.

Chapter One

Copy and Pivot

Good businesses don't spring to life fully formed. Inspiration gets them started, but the ones that survive are shaped by constant research, innovation and adaptation.

At around the age of eight or nine, I started tying the flies that anglers use to fish for trout and salmon. For some reason I found fly-tying more enjoyable than collecting stamps or kicking a ball about. I had a friend, Nick Whitehouse, who was a fisherman, and he showed me how to assemble the flies. He also showed me how to fish, but I never took to it: tying the flies was far more interesting.

What I found even more compelling was the business of selling my ties to friends, to fishing tackle shops and at village shows. This is the point at which I discovered the joys of business research. It'll come as no great shock if I tell you that Britain's fly-tying industry was something less than a model of chromed efficiency. The tackle shops knew they were serving a hobby market, so they overcharged for fly-tying gear but undercharged for completed flies so they could compete with the mail-order companies. These companies weren't much to write home about, though, always advertising items that were very often out of stock.

If I just sold the flies I made back to the tackle shops that sold me the gear, then I'd lose money. The only way I'd make money was to become a wholesaler, and this I did, to the frustration of my chemistry teacher (I used to bunk off his lessons to go and pay in cheques or talk to the bank manager).

Bit by bit, I learned to innovate. I called myself Fly-Tying Tackle Products, which at least had the virtue of clarity, and – exhibiting wisdom beyond my years – I decided I'd better do even more market research before I went all-in on the idea. A twenty-word advertisement in *Trout & Salmon*, the sport's monthly magazine, cost me £8, and enough people replied asking for my catalogue to convince me that I should put one together. This I did, in a white heat, and with apologies for 'having run out of stock' of a catalogue that didn't yet exist.

If you ever need a crash course in supply chain management, set up a fly-tying business. The best flies are made from cockerels' capes – stiff feathers that make the fly stand up on top of the water. Quality is really important, and feathers from India are excellent – only I had to send them to Rentokil first to be fumigated, because they were riddled with bugs. Annoyed by the unplanned expense, I decided to do my own fumigation. I got hold of an old chest freezer and bought some formaldehyde, masks and white coats. My mother's £100 loan was looking pretty depleted by then, but by delivering on my offer of a return-of-post service, I achieved a first-year turnover of over £1,500, of which £356 was profit. So far, so good.

The next year I took Fly-Tying Tackle Products to the National Game Fair, and it was there that I learned the importance of adaptation. This three-day event pulled in around 150,000 visitors from the hunting, shooting and fishing set. My friend Nick, who was older and had a driving licence, drove the Transit van. With Nick, my brother Stephen (smarter and more handsome than me) and a few more friends, I'd camp in a farmer's field on the way, have a few tins of beer and smoke cigarettes. Somewhere behind us, our parents were following in the caravan. Determined to shell out on a good education for us, this was about as much of a holiday as we ever got.

The fair was one long enjoyable lesson in retail, for a boy who had never found long lessons particularly enjoyable. I learned what sold and what didn't, I learned which products I was missing and I picked up very quickly on the importance of store layout and clear pricing.

The following year, I doubled my sales and profits. The next year, they doubled again. This was no accident: I was constantly chipping away at things: better pricing, better signage, better labelling and

– now that I was paying people – better staff. With dollar signs in my eyes, I changed the name of the company – Quali-Tye was much more distinctive than Fly-Tying Tackle Products – and thought I was due a spot of plain sailing.

A chance remark, overheard on the stall, changed all that and triggered another cycle of innovation. 'Oooh! They'd make nice earrings.' A few of the fishermen's wives and girlfriends had gathered round the big purple flies I'd been making – the ones with an ostrich feather built in. Where I saw fishing tackle, they saw fashion items. I wish all market research was so simple.

This revelation inspired a significant change in direction for Quali-Tye. The business outgrew my bedroom and had to move into an outbuilding. My mother was looking after the mail-order business with help from a couple of part-time employees, and we began importing flies from Nakuru in Kenya. They arrived with barbs attached, naturally, and our job was to sit there with wire cutters, cutting the barbs off so they could be made into earrings. I hired a bunch of outworkers in York, and would dash around on a bicycle delivering them the kidney wires to put on the hooks. We put the finished articles into bags, labelled them and fixed them onto display cards ready for delivery to hair salons. Placed next to the till, they proved an irresistible impulse buy for teenage girls.

Already a product of research, innovation and adaptation, Quali-Tye was an excellent business. All it lacked, as it pivoted from fishing to fashion, was an excellent name. A government-paid marketing consultant pooh-poohed my own suggestion, 'Danglers', saying it inferred something unseemly and organic. He suggested I call my earrings something much more tasteful: how about 'Hookers'?

Within a week we'd been featured on radio and TV and in just about every national newspaper, and soon I was ringing up big department stores in London: 'I'm coming down on Tuesday 22nd to see Harrods, and I wonder if I could pop in and see you as well . . .?'

THE COMPETITION KNOWS MORE THAN YOU DO

Starting a successful business so young gave me a singular advantage: humility. Being 'just a kid', I could never assume that I was cleverer than my competition. I've nurtured that attitude. The guys lurking round the corner are, I am sure, powered by some secret sauce. The only way I'm going to succeed is by being more energetic and more determined than them.

From this comes an insight I've clung to throughout my business life: there must surely be something I can learn from my competition. And that's what my colleagues and I did, continually, as we developed my two best-known businesses, HomeServe and Checkatrade.

We watched our competitors. We even *consulted* our competitors, and openly emulated whatever we saw worked well for them. And because we paid attention, and spent our time taking notes and knocking on doors and being friendly and fair (while others wasted their time behind closed doors, poring over their vision statements), we managed to outcompete, outmanoeuvre and, over the course of years, out-evolve every competitor.

You may recall that Netflix, an innovative and successful streaming company, began life by copying Blockbuster. They copied what worked from Blockbuster, and then assessed what the market wanted and how the business could be improved. Sometimes, as an entrepreneur, it helps to be a small step behind the curve. We can still be innovators and pioneers, but we also want to develop our skills as students of the market.

We are taught at school that copying is bad. This is not true in business. Taking personal credit for someone else's work *is* bad, obviously, but copying is simply how we learn. And by adapting someone else's good idea, you can turn it into a brand new offering.

I got talking about this with Touker Suleyman, a British entrepreneur and investor best known for his appearances on the TV show *Dragons' Den*. He's the owner of fashion brand Hawes & Curtis and womenswear label Ghost, and has a long history of successful retail and manufacturing ventures. Touker has never lost sight of the fundamental simplicity that underpins all business. 'You don't have to be a genius to start a business. You don't have to be a rocket scientist. You don't have to invent anything new. All you've got to do is take a product, look at it, and make it better. Change it. Take an off-the-shelf product and adapt it. Simple as that.

'Somebody came to me this week with a pair of sneaker trees,' Touker told me.

'As in—'

'As in shoe trees for sneakers. What's so great about that? Well, there are, for a start, the over 1.2 billion pairs of sneakers being sold across the world every year. And that sneaker tree could be sold anywhere in the world. It's not expensive to make. The moulds are expensive, and they're what I've invested in, because once you've got the moulds, there's no more design to do. You might want to ring in a few colour changes to refresh the item now and again, but essentially you just need to turn the product out at scale.'

You're probably thinking, if business were that simple then we'd all be tycoons. But I can promise you, it's not complexity that makes business difficult. Rather, it's the ease with which your eyes can come unglued from the ball. Human beings have evolved to be easily distracted, and entrepreneurs, in their pursuit of shiny new things, are some of the most easily distracted people on the planet.

Staying focused on the customer and the customer's changing needs sounds easy, but it's genuinely hard to do, especially as a business grows and acquires a more complex structure.

One industry that produces very complex goods came up with a way of doing business that deliberately baked customer feedback into their sales model. I know software development can be its own can of worms, but you do have to hand it to the industry for biting the bullet and accepting that they had to release their wares even as they were improving upon them. If your ambition is to develop something that's absolutely extraordinary, you can't afford not to test it as you go. You may want to keep version 1.0 of your idea to a small group of friends; but, equally, you don't want to be haemorrhaging research-and-development money all the way to version 6.3, only to discover your product is not quite what the customer wants or needs.

Innovation is about getting your idea 80 per cent right – in other words, to the point where the business case is solid and you know you're not going to lose your shirt. After that, the best ideas for improvement are most likely to come from your customers.

The continued success of open-source software demonstrates the wisdom of 'copy and pivot'. Take what's out there and fit it to a new purpose. There's really no need to reinvent the wheel, and there are certainly no awards going for people who do. 'One thing we've got today which we didn't have when I started out is the internet,' Touker Suleyman reflects, 'and though it's a maddening distraction a lot of the time, it feels almost purpose-built for those heady early days of company creation. Within seconds, you can see your competition. I spend a lot of time on my iPad at night looking at companies and what they're up to. If somebody comes in with an idea, I will search to see who their competitors are. There's no longer any excuse for sloppy or thin research.'

My friend and first investor, Simon Blunt – who you will hear about often in the course of this book – is a director of several companies related to property and finance. In 1997, he founded the Mortgage Advice Bureau, a major player in the UK mortgage market. It connects borrowers with lenders, helping people find the best mortgage deals to suit their needs. But he didn't invent it out of whole cloth. He copied the business model of the franchise company I had been working with.

'People's idea of a mortgage broker back then was someone above a betting shop who would rip you off,' Simon recalls, 'and what I wanted to do was to set up in town centres and give the whole operation the feel of a building society – or at the very least a place that wasn't going to fleece you.'

The trouble was, he couldn't make any money out of it. Together, Simon and I hashed out a business model that involved franchising the business out to estate agents.

Estate agents sell houses, and they do some surveying for banks and building societies, but they don't like doing mortgages, because the compliance is a pain and quite a serious drain on their time. They give you the impression they do it only because it's another thing that brings customers through the door.

The pivot point for Simon came when he realised that he'd been looking at estate agents all wrong. Like most people, he had assumed the estate agents made all the money, and the mortgage business was just this slightly unwelcome house guest. When you looked into the numbers, though, you could see that the reality was exactly the opposite: it was the mortgage side that made the money! 'The estate agency was really just a fancy shop window.'

That's why we thought we could franchise Simon's business to estate agents. They already employed the staff Simon needed, but his company could support them and run all their financial services for them.

Simon takes up the story: 'I took this idea to Legal & General with Rick Palmer, who was my business partner at the time. Legal & General was responsible for the insurance packages that estate agents sold along with their mortgages. We were a very small broker, and our CVs were not particularly impressive. My first job had been castrating cattle in Australia. Around the same time, Rick had been collecting deckchairs on Brighton beach.'

I remember this: they brought me along to the meeting because, though at the time I was no one's idea of a heavy hitter, I'd at least worked for Procter & Gamble. (They had to trust that I wouldn't mention being a stage magician or selling rabbits.)

I can't remember how much use I was, but Simon and Rick walked out with so much new business it took a while to sink in. Their turnover was about £50,000: Legal & General offered them half a million pounds. That was a lot of money in 1994.

The editor-in-chief of the magazine I own, *Business Leader*, is Graham Ruddick, the former deputy business editor of *The Times*. As he points out, 'Publishing, at least the way we do it, is entirely a copy-and-pivot business. We learn as we go. We put content out into the world and get feedback.'

The change he's just now seeing through, as I write this, is to use illustrations instead of portraits on the front cover. 'If you look at WHSmith, you will be hit by a wave of faces, so illustrations actually stand out much more on the racks. The other problem with faces is that you've got to know who these people are before you'll pick up the magazine. Very few business people have much rock-star familiarity about them.'

At my investment company Growth Partner, meanwhile, I work closely with businesses serving very fast-moving, fashion-driven markets. No business without a culture of 'copy and pivot' could survive more than a few months in that environment.

One of the most able operators in that market is Victoria Lynch, the founder of haircare products company Additional Lengths. (We invested in her business in 2021.) She left school with no qualifications to work as a machine operator in the local factory, while training to be a hairdresser at nights and weekends. The company she built now supplies thousands of salons, and I've backed her to expand into America.

'Our industry is driven by trends,' she says, 'so we have to be adaptable. I see this even within our own team. Someone might say, "I just bought this amazing product," only for someone else to reply, "I wouldn't be caught dead wearing *that*." '

Whereas her competitors tend to focus on few products and innovate slowly, Victoria's business caters for many different customers and is laser-focused on their changing needs. 'Women in their twenties and thirties are often focused on building their careers and personal brands. They care about how they present themselves. They're willing to invest in high-quality hair extensions that will last. But, of course, not everyone has the same level of disposable income, so we offer a range of products to fit different budgets, from affordable clip-in extensions for occasional use to premium, long-lasting options.'

Victoria works closely with suppliers, testing the products herself and even developing new colours. 'I do see the value in "copying and pivoting",' she says, 'but it's a bit different when you're the one leading the way, and others are copying you! We often set the trends in our industry. When we launch a new colour, our competitors will try to copy it. One company in particular is notorious for this: they blatantly copy our products but try to disguise the fact by giving their copies fancy names. We have a popular shade called "613" – that's the standard colour code hair stylists use. We like using numbers because it highlights our transparency and our commitment to the professional end of the market. Our competitors call their copy "Dubai".

'The point, I think, is not to copy others slavishly but to copy in pursuit of your own innovation. If I'm not convinced by a new product, we might let a competitor launch it first. They'll often make mistakes or overlook key aspects. Then we swoop in with a better version and capitalise on their missteps.'

The Covid-19 pandemic triggered an altogether more profound period of change for Victoria's company, and involved a complex and difficult pivot from a primarily wholesale business to a mostly retail one.

'Covid had a major impact on us,' she recalls. 'We were in the process of moving our warehouse, and we had to put everything on hold – no deliveries, no collections, nothing. We actually shut down our website for a while. It stayed closed for seven months. Our trade professionals, the salons, were closed, so our online revenue completely dried up.

'We decided to stop online sales completely for several months. Everyone was supposed to be staying home, and we didn't want to be complicit in any activity that put people at risk. When we finally reopened the website, we saw a surge in orders for removal tools and solutions. Many stylists had applied hair extensions before the lockdown, and their clients needed to remove them safely at home, because even when pubs were allowed to reopen in July 2020, salons remained closed for another month.

'Recovery was slow. People weren't going out, attending events or socialising, so they didn't need our products. Our revenue plummeted. When the salons were finally able to reopen, we had to operate under strict restrictions. We were cleaning and sterilising constantly, wearing masks and disposable aprons. It felt like we were running a medical facility.

'This whole experience made us realise that we were missing out on a huge opportunity in the consumer market. We had been so focused on serving professionals that we had neglected everyday consumers. We needed to change our approach.

'So, we started working on ways to attract and engage with consumers. We're trying to convert customers from other brands and build a loyal following. We know it will be challenging, because consumers tend to be less loyal than trade professionals, but the best way to build a customer's loyalty is to understand their needs and provide solutions, so we'll take it one step at a time.'

THE MORE MISTAKES, THE BETTER

HomeServe, which was eventually valued at over £4 billion, evolved slowly from a series of tiny 'copy and pivot' experiments that commenced almost the moment I left York University.

I had written my undergraduate dissertation on how manufacturing companies set their prices. I'd focused on businesses in Newton Aycliffe in Durham, and I wasn't especially bowled over by what I had discovered. In answer to the question, 'How do you determine price?' every single business came back with the same answer: 'We buy at this price, we add on a [usually 10 per cent] mark-up, and sell at this price' – in other words, 'cost-plus'.

This seemed to me a painfully crude way of going about things. From my own fly-tying business, I could see that it would be much better to ask the customer what they would be prepared to pay. The whole point of business is to add value. When it comes to measuring how much value you're adding, are you really going to just pluck a number out of the air?

York's degree course in economics was very good, but in all honesty I got more out of my membership of the Student Industrial Society. We visited local businesses, and there I experienced close-up how companies operated, the way staff collaborated, the conditions they worked under, the techniques used by management. These live tutorials were far more valuable than lectures back on campus.

Some visits were more enjoyable than others. A day out at Samuel Smith's brewery in Tadcaster passed in a pleasant blur. Wandering through a Buxted chicken factory was gripping, from an industrial point of view, but stomach churning: like most people, I suspect, I didn't like thinking about where meat comes from.

And all the while, I was still running Quali-Tye, fielding customer enquiries from as far away as the US. I acquired some notoriety at university for convincing British Telecom that it had to give me a phone. This involved laying a mile and a half of fresh line to my room at Wentworth, my hall of residence, at a cost of who knows how many thousands of pounds, all for its fixed price of £49. If you phoned my office and the answerphone told you, 'The office is currently unmanned', it meant I was in lectures.

I got my comeuppance for being so flash a year later, while sharing a house on Wellington Street with three girls. I got myself over-committed and didn't have time to do the washing-up before I had to run and catch a National Express coach. I hid the dirty pans in a cupboard, ran around the country selling Hookers earrings to hair salons, got home, opened the cupboard, found it empty, thought to myself, 'I'm in for it now', fell into bed – and guess where all the pans had ended up?

In my third year I lined up a job with Deloitte in Newcastle. My father was delighted: I'd be earning a safe business qualification and pulling down a regular salary. But I doubt he was very surprised when I announced I had come across an advert on the noticeboard outside my economics lecture theatre and had found myself something much more interesting to do.

'Three days of fun in Newcastle in a Holiday Inn' was how Procter & Gamble pitched its three-day marketing vocation course. Maybe it intended a little light irony; the fact is, I had a great time. I was a complete outlier – the nearest thing to a Newcastle native among a dozen Oxbridge types – and so I got to show my cohort around the town. We all pitched in wonderfully well, at work and out of it, and when the chance came to stay on as a brand assistant at P&G's Newcastle headquarters, I seized it.

Brand assistants learned everything about how to make a product successful. We got a crash course in packaging, marketing, advertising, pricing, manufacturing and promotions – and P&G even paid us for our trouble.

For most businesses, marketing is the engine for growth, and to be successful at it, you need to track and measure everything. One of the key things we did was rigorously test our TV advertising campaigns. Before launching nationwide, we'd run the ads in smaller, localised markets. We studied the results to see how effective the campaign was in driving sales. Each brand (mine was Fairy Liquid detergent) was handled by a small, team-led business within the larger P&G enterprise. The accelerated learning I received there was better than any university course. The evenings and weekends were just as important: when we socialised, we went on talking about work and exchanging ideas. We were constantly learning from each other. There were thirteen of us: a ready-made peer group. The most effective training model is the one that never stops.

Over three and a half years, between 1986 and 1990, I championed Fairy Liquid and Camay soap, and one not very famous brand, Vortex bleach. We ran all manner of experiments and trials; I remember I persuaded Gruner + Jahr, the publishers of *Prima* magazine – a leading, if not *the* leading women's magazine at the time – to send out free copies to people who sent us the caps from Fairy Liquid bottles. I'd persuaded Gruner + Jahr to bear all the costs, and their magazine was worth more than our detergent, but the idea must have paid off for them, because soon you saw offers like that everywhere.

Best of all, I found myself in a company that truly cared about what the customer was thinking and feeling. This validated what I had always suspected: that you should always run a business with the end consumer in mind, setting prices according to what your customers will pay, and reaping the rewards of adding value, rather than just adding an arbitrary margin to what something cost to manufacture.

Soon enough I was promoted to brand manager. I had sold Quali-Tye, but I had lost none of my appetite for running my own business, and Procter & Gamble positively encouraged entrepreneurial thinking.

Not every experiment paid off. The Christmas tree project involved me selling Christmas trees in pub car parks – only this seriously annoyed the greengrocers who drank in the pubs. They had to pay ground rent on their lots, so why was this lad allowed to sell trees in the car park? I'd just brought in a couple of big consignments of trees, and suddenly I found myself chucked off my selling sites. I had to get up before dawn and go to the wholesale fruit-and-veg market to sell them in bulk, before coming in and doing a full day's work at P&G; then till midnight I'd be delivering trees that had been ordered house to house.

It was a P&G colleague, Richard Johns, who inspired my next business, providing freshers at different universities with their own one-off student magazine, which would serve as a guide to the town or city they'd be living in for the next three years.

Richard and I ran our publishing business from my converted garage-office at my house in Gosforth, which I'd bought on the proceeds of Quali-Tye's sale. It was a frenetic time – my house was itself a business, as I was renting out the other two bedrooms and the dining room to three other young professionals at £40 a week.

Our magazine was called *Connect*, and though it was only ever meant to be a one-off venture, it was sufficiently consuming that it taught me an abiding lesson in salesmanship: without an element of salesmanship, you can barely begin to have an impact on the market. I learned this the hard way, sitting in my converted garage, flogging advertising space to Sainsbury's, Dixons and other major national companies.

My friend, the British entrepreneur and investor Jeremy Middleton – who will also become a regular feature of these tales – makes a similar, but rather broader point: 'It's all about execution. To get a winning concept, you've got to be good at execution. To get it out there into the world, you've got to be good at execution. If you're not good at execution, you're never going to be much good at anything. Everyone's got this idea that you can walk into a lift and three seconds later, you've got the money. It doesn't happen.'

Jeremy's my go-to business partner, one of my oldest friends, and godfather to Jemima, my oldest child. (Wonderfully, he asked me to return the favour when his first was born.) Most everything else I did while still at Procter & Gamble, I did jointly with Jeremy; he'd joined Procter & Gamble a couple of years before me, and it was in his team that I wrestled (as it were) with Zest soap and Fairy Liquid.

Jeremy was another outlier at Procter & Gamble; he'd scraped into Kent University and had been working in a clearing bank ('I was dreadful at it and they hated me') when by chance he read about Procter & Gamble's graduate programme. They took a few mavericks each year, and Jeremy and I hit it off very quickly, bonding over our shared determination to one day run our own businesses.

Then Jeremy got an offer to go to Egypt for a year and become Procter & Gamble's marketing manager there. He already had his own business, which involved applying for a 100 per cent mortgage (remember them?), renting out rooms and effectively getting a free house – a 'buy to let' business, in other words, though the idea had yet to catch on. He had a few houses he was letting out to young professionals, room by room: the one he lived in, his girlfriend's house and one other he had bought. He had lined someone up to look after things while he was away, but at the last minute they let him down. I was more than happy to step into the breach, and by the time Jeremy got back from Cairo I'd bought three or four houses myself.

This property letting business was our first collaboration, and even with the pair of us working full tilt, it wasn't easy to juggle our full-time jobs at Procter & Gamble with our own business.

Hard work forged an inseparable bond between us. On a handshake, we agreed that we would split gains, losses, salaries, everything. We were already buying houses, but property businesses take a long time to grow and require a lot of capital. Anyway, we were impatient – so we pivoted from property investment to property management.

We were both keen to get some experience as business consultants, and I did some work in the marketing department of Coopers &

Lybrand in Newcastle. Jeremy wrapped up his work with P&G and went to work for PricewaterhouseCoopers. We spent a little bit of our time consulting and a lot of time thinking about what we were going to do by ourselves. By then we had ten houses, with five tenants in each, which generated just enough mayhem to make it hard to hold down another job.

So I quit, and we settled into a pattern where Jeremy would work all hours pulling down a good wage from PwC, and I would work all hours commuting to and from Albert Road in Middlesbrough (not the sexiest place to be) and losing everything we had on lots of under-capitalised early-stage businesses, none of which worked very well.

We needed maintenance people to look after our properties, and this led to other things – an ironing service, a repair and maintenance business, an interior design and decorating company, a spell as a franchisee in a chain of mortgage shops . . .

With hindsight, of course, you can see how these businesses laid the foundation for the billion-pound business that would follow. But, the truth is, Jeremy and I tried to make some of these businesses work for quite a long time, and even if they bumbled along making a little bit of money, we weren't really finding the 'Big Idea'. 'We would have focused earlier if we could have,' Jeremy recalls, 'and we must have gone through ten different businesses – some dumber than others. But you don't know until you try, and if we'd focused on any one of them, it wouldn't have worked. The successful model just wasn't there.'

Our letting agency business, Professional Properties, remained a kitchen-table operation. We'd walk the length of Shields Road in Byker, Newcastle, looking for the cheapest goods we could find to furnish and equip our properties. Jeremy remembers us competing over who could negotiate the best price for a pack of forks.

The one act of largesse we allowed ourselves was to find a bigger table to work at. This belonged to our first employee, the excellent Jane Dixon. It's still a source of mild embarrassment to me that we hired her, first of all, for her table. We'd placed an ad in the paper and went round to people's houses to interview them, claiming that we liked to interview people in their own homes because it gave us a better idea of what they were like. The truth is, we didn't have an office to invite them to.

Jane very generously agreed to let us use her home as an office and her lounge as the place where young professionals came to see what properties were available. Our weekly meeting, every Saturday morning, took place in her kitchen.

Pivoting from property investment to property management, we started providing a service for other landlords. We ended up managing six hundred properties. Our biggest problem – and it got exponentially bigger with every new property we managed – was when tenants called on a Friday evening to report a blocked drain, or water pouring out of a radiator, or a broken-down boiler. Jane was often on the sharp end of these calls and found she couldn't get a Geordie plumber out at unsociable hours for love nor money.

Jeremy and I were at a national franchise exhibition when we spotted a business that seemed a heaven-sent solution: First Call ran a network of guys in yellow vans and promised a twenty-four-hour, one-hour call-out domestic emergency service covering all trades.

And if we desperately needed their services, surely others must? We had some discussions with First Call about becoming their franchisee, but in the end we figured we might as well try the business model for ourselves. We got ourselves two hired vans and two plumbers, and set up our own business. Our home repair and maintenance business, FastFix (soon rechristened A1 FastFix to put it top of the Yellow Pages directory listing), operated from the same kitchen table as everything else.

After the first full year of trading – or perhaps the first accounting period – we discovered that Jeremy had made £100,000 from his management consultancy work, and I had lost £100,000 through FastFix.

'We spent all the money we didn't have,' Jeremy remembers, 'and then we spent all the tenants' deposits, which these days would land us in prison. In those days, so long as you repaid them – which we always did – you were in the clear. But we had no cash.'

We had poured our life savings into FastFix, imagining that a phone book listing would be enough to create a profitable business. We got a good number of calls, but once we were paid for a job, that was the last we heard from that customer, at least until their next breakdown, which might not happen for years. We were haemorrhaging all our money on advertising, trying to attract customers who, after just one transaction, had no compelling reason to remember us.

We liked the kind of business we were in. We liked helping people. I especially liked the fact that each day, we brought a little island of calm to someone who might be standing, stressed out, in inches of water. (When HomeServe got big, I still found time to listen in on our call-centre conversations, 'ensuring high levels of customer service', of course, but also to remind myself of the company's founding magic.)

So here was the challenge facing Jeremy and me: how could our emergency property repairs company attract recurring revenue?

Through the Marketing Department, the consultancy he had set up for us, Jeremy pitched FastFix to some water companies. The UK water industry was being privatised at the time and was looking for ways to diversify. Jeremy's consultancy provided help for companies that didn't have their own marketing departments. He said to them: 'Why don't we look at setting up a plumbing business?'

Our original proposition was to offer the UK's water companies a pay-on-use emergency plumbing service. This was a reasonable business idea, but it wasn't necessarily one that appealed to companies whose interest in their product typically ended at the stopcock.

For the longest time, the water companies had existed primarily to own the infrastructure. They dictated to customers what they could and could not do and what they should pay, and still weren't thinking like commercial organisations. Rather than thinking, 'How can we delight the customer so that they want to spend more with us?', their philosophy was, 'How do we extract the most profit from our monopoly?'

Jeremy and I got some board-level responses from maybe half a dozen companies, but in the end South Staffordshire Water, one of the smallest outfits, was the only one to commission us to study the idea. This was Jeremy's first commission as an independent consultant and it was a tiny job. South Staffs was based in Walsall and envisaged setting up a small, regional, direct-labour plumbing operation. Through Jeremy's recommendation, South Staffs employed me on a consultancy basis to run the numbers. It was a six-week job, worth about £4,500.

Further study confirmed what Jeremy and I already suspected: running a plumbing business was a great idea in principle, but an ordinary, direct-labour plumbing business wasn't going to work. The company needed to go national with a franchise model, offering emergency cover at a premium price.

South Staffs was a 'heritage' company, formed by an Act of Parliament in 1853 to supply clean water to the people of the Black Country. The board enjoyed wine with its lunches. Once a year the higher-ups would go to visit a pumping station or something, and there was a big performance around it all. So, an entrepreneurial new business venture would require entrepreneurial incomers to run it. 'The good news,' we explained to South Staffs's finance director Steve Coathup, 'is we know where you can get the outfit you need – and what's more, it's free.'

We would put in a small test operation, A1 FastFix. South Staffs would provide the working capital we needed and the brand name; and we'd split the business fifty-fifty.

It was a good pitch, but let's be frank: we were desperate, and were effectively offering South Staffs fully half our business, if only they would provide us with a bit of working capital. And, being not so daft, that's what they did.

MANY SMALL FAVOURS (AND ONE BIG MISTAKE)

For a flavour of what South Staffs was like, there's no better person to ask than Anna Maughan. She began her career there in 1998, joining HomeServe only when we demerged in 2004. For the next twenty-five years, she was part of our family, our company secretary from

2008 and a member of our executive committee from 2020 until the takeover in 2023.

'My role at South Staffs was cobbled together over time,' Anna remembers. 'To begin with, the finance director gave me the company's pensions to look after, so I built up some expertise and the job was never really reassigned. The company's structure wasn't wildly strange, but where it evolved to work well, we didn't interfere with it. A new finance director came in and appointed me company secretary, but I kept on being handed slightly odd things, like looking after the trademarks. Despite being a listed company, South Staffs wasn't a large organisation. We didn't do "investor relations" – we just talked to people. We were a small company, growing at a decent clip.'

This rather gives the lie to the idea that South Staffs was a bit of a dinosaur. 'But if you mean that South Staffs felt very old-fashioned, you have a point. I can remember in the early days, when HomeServe was recruiting younger staff for their call centres, some of the older water company staff used to comment on what the HomeServe lot were wearing. When HomeServe organised events or they hit a sales target there was all this cheering and clapping – behaviour completely alien to people just serving customers in the water company.'

No entrepreneur is terribly good at the detail. All entrepreneurs need people to sort out the carnage they leave in their wake. I learned from the outset to hire people who were brilliant at this, and Jennifer Synnott was an early win. She'd been at South Staffs for five or six years when FastFix arrived, and her services were mine for the asking. I gave her the strangest (and possibly the most inept) interview of her career – I wouldn't stop talking – but it worked out well in the end: she remained a central and essential part of our operation until 2009.

She can remember when HomeServe (well, FastFix – the HomeServe idea was still a way off) consisted of a few temporary staff and a three-legged table – that is, a four-legged table with one leg missing. It just about stood up, which was as well since we opened all our letters and application forms there. 'We'd been given an office – well, more of a cupboard, really – which had a surprising number of doors. We sealed all but two of them and took the handles off so we'd have a bit more room to move around.'

South Staffs's telecoms manager set up some phones for us, and the IT manager organised a little software system to run the business. Every once in a while we got a bit of management support. These all felt like small favours, but over time they added up to a constant stream of practical support for what we were doing. You can't underestimate the value of that, and it's more the kind of backing you'd expect from a private equity house.

I didn't have much to offer to the people South Staffs released to me. I was in no position to offer them any kind of career path. But I did have a story to tell, and a vision to sell. Jennifer was in her early twenties. She'd done her MBA, had worked a few years with South Staffs and was hungry for more business experience. 'I suppose it was a little bit of a gamble,' she remembers. 'There wasn't really anything other than passion and enthusiasm – but the atmosphere was infectious.'

We had ambitious growth plans and, fuelled by South Staffs's £100,000 investment, achieved 20 per cent year-on-year growth. No mean feat, that – though we still weren't making any money. In fact we were making a loss of – oh, what a coincidence! – £100,000.

All the while we were being held together by Jennifer, who was putting the operation together, instilling discipline, trying to control a platform that would deliver our vision. I mistakenly thought that if we grew revenue fast, we would get significant economies of scale, which would lead to profitability. It didn't, and it won't. For companies that haven't yet proven their business model, this kind of strategy will only increase their losses, no matter how effectively they scale up.

Instead of getting economies of scale as my emergency plumbing business grew, the break-even line got further and further away, and monthly losses increased from £10,000 to £50,000 a month. 'There was this elusive break-even point,' Jeremy recalls. 'How were we going to get there? The answer couldn't be by continuing to roll out a model that didn't work.'

I look back at this experience as one of my most important lessons: you can't expand a business into profit. If you can't make something work on a small scale, all that will happen on a bigger scale is that it will lose more money.

THEIR PROBLEMS ARE YOUR BUSINESS

It's amusing now to look back at the cultural differences between us and South Staffs. I think they found me a rather strange chap. Rolling up in a Porsche on day one probably didn't do me many favours. (I quickly switched to a rather clapped-out Rover.) Culturally, you couldn't imagine two more different sets of people. The board was made up of old gentleman farmers who arrived at meetings in their Rolls-Royces. But they were smart – smart enough to see straight away that they couldn't run us like a water company. Brian Whitty, who became South Staffs's CFO and then chief executive, deserves credit for managing us and for giving us just enough rope to play with, but never quite enough to hang ourselves.

'South Staffs didn't exactly drown us in cash,' Jeremy remembers, 'and less than two years later we were saying to each other, "Oh, Christ. We're going to go bust again."

'Then came the pivot: we thought, "Why aren't we selling to the 85 per cent of people who don't have plumbing emergencies, rather than to the 15 per cent who do?"'

FastFix was a hard business. It's hard to make money to do the marketing, to find jobs, and then to go and quote for the job, and then do the job, and then pay everyone for doing it, and then try to collect the money. If, on the other hand, you sell people peace of mind against a plumbing emergency, then 85 per cent of those people are just paying money upfront for a claim that doesn't happen.

Back at university (and through a friend, Nick Duxbury, if I'm remembering this correctly), I had come across the story of Patsy Bloom, who founded the Petplan Group in the 1970s. Her dog was sick, with a history of illness, and she was haemorrhaging money on vets' fees, when she hit upon the idea of a health insurance scheme for animals. She found a business partner, and they each invested £250 into the new venture. Sixteen years later, Bloom's business had a turnover of £20 million. She later sold out to Cornhill Insurance (later Allianz) for £32.5 million – a near 65,000-fold return on her initial investment.

There's no such thing as a good idea out of nowhere; it needed the pieces of the puzzle to come together in our heads before we could say we had 'invented' plumbing and drainage warranties. And that, of course, was only the start. Next came the hard work of adapting, innovating, challenging and testing.

Plenty of people had tried to offer roughly the kind of service we were evolving, but they hadn't got the model quite right. South Staffs Water used to mail out an application form from Green Flag in each household bill. It wasn't a bad offer on paper. Green Flag were offering to repair everything around the house – roof repair, plumbing, electrics, the lot – for between £100 and £110.

When you took that leaflet into a focus group, though, people would say either 'That's too good to be true' or 'I've got some of those things covered already, and I don't want to pay twice'. Some people said, 'Who the hell are Green Flag?'

We stripped down the offer so that at the very least it seemed relevant to the customer. Because we only covered your plumbing, naturally the price we were charging was much lower – around £50.

We were down to our last £10,000, with friends and family urging me to give up on my entrepreneur dream and return to Procter & Gamble, when, by chance, we stumbled on the final piece of the jigsaw. Sutton Water, another small water company in the south, ran a successful plumbing insurance business. We found out all we could about them and hastily assembled a focus group of Sutton's customers in the local Holiday Inn.

We asked them: Why did you join? What do you like about Sutton's warranty? What don't you like about it? We took out the bits they didn't like, like the annual inspection of the underground water pipe, and we added in drainage cover and internal plumbing emergency cover.

People's main worry, and what had made them sign up, was that they had no idea what to do if a leak sprang in the pipe connecting their property to the mains supply. They liked Sutton's product because, while their household insurance policies said they were covered for water damage, Sutton were the only ones willing to pay to fix the actual leak.

But there was, we discovered, another anxiety that Sutton's policy did not address. These connecting pipes often run under walls, lawns and driveways, so repairing them isn't really a repair you'd entrust to just anybody. The people in our focus group worried about the damage that might be done to their property.

This was our 'in'. Our warranty, we decided, wouldn't just cover your repair bill – it would promise that whoever came out to you in an emergency (and they'd be someone qualified and highly rated) would finish up properly and not leave great holes in your wall or your lawn. Indeed, we'd indemnify you against that risk.

Finally, since we were working with the water company, and nobody outside the water company knew who we were, we made a deal to put the water company's name on our literature. Like most people, I can't honestly say that I like my water company. Unless there's a problem, I rarely ever think about them. But do I trust them to know when there's a leak and be able to fix it? Well, yes, I think I do.

After so long turning a small loss-making repairs business into a big loss-making repairs business, Jeremy and I were rapidly running out of rope. We started testing on a small scale, focusing on direct mail and carefully measuring our results (a very 'Procter & Gamble' approach). Meanwhile I kept my mind off imminent disaster by imagining what would happen if everything worked out well. The way I saw it, if we could only prove our idea with one little water company, we could do affinity deals with all the other water companies. Sometimes they might want to take our idea and do it themselves, but that didn't matter: since this was all we did, day in day out, week after week, we'd be far better at it than they were. And once the idea was proven in the UK, we could do deals around the world!

And all the while, our twenty-three employees were facing almost immediate redundancy, waiting for the results of our little experiment.

Now, what you need to know at this point is that a direct mail campaign expects to get about a 1 per cent take-up. If you get a 1.5 per cent take-up, you're doing well. For our experiment, we had sent out just 1,000 leaflets – and got thirty-eight replies. Doesn't sound much, does it? But look again: it's a take-up rate of 3.8 per cent.

The smaller your sample, the less certain you can be about your result. We ran the experiment again to make sure this wasn't a fluke. This time, we sent out 100,000 leaflets. And, sure enough, the take-up rate was the same. And I mean *exactly* the same: 3.8 per cent on the button! It was uncanny.

I climbed up on my desk in front of a couple of dozen very anxious employees and made the announcement: 'Yes,' I said, 'we've made it.' You can never predict with absolute certainty how a business will grow. What you can say, though, is that whatever works in 1,000 households stands a good chance of working in 100,000 households, and what works hundreds of thousands of times is likely to work many millions of times. At the end of our second year, our new company, Home Service Scheme, had over 100,000 customers in the West Midlands and had increased its turnover to £3.67 million, turning a first-year loss into a profit of £700,000.

The following year, we signed our first affinity partnership agreement with Anglian Water. We had 225,000 members now and had doubled turnover to £7.2 million. By the end of the 1997/98 financial year, we had half a million members, had doubled turnover again to £14 million and signed affinity partnerships with most other major water companies in England. This contributed an operating profit of nearly £5 million to the South Staffs accounts – approximately 30 per cent of the group's total operating profit.

And we carried on testing and improving. For instance, we expanded our offering to cover plumbing maintenance like dripping taps. We also improved our communications with the water companies. These were traditionally risk-averse businesses, suddenly desperate for other sources of income. They lived in fear of reputational damage and in terror of the regulator, Ofwat. They were also under considerable pressure to cut costs. Jennifer Synnott was our ambassador to these companies, effectively saying to them, 'Don't worry, these guys might be a bit scary – ex-Procter & Gamble marketeers are a very different animal to you – but I'm the same animal as you, and I'm the one who's going to see this deal through.'

Our 'affinity marketing' offer involved selling plumbing insurance under the water company's name, in return for a fee. If you bought an 'Anglian' policy, for example, you were actually buying from us. Anglian not only got a fee but also the reputational boost that came from our plumbers and engineers doing a good job. (It goes without saying that this entire business depended on HomeServe's engineers being at the top of their game.)

We thought about taking on the risk of our warranties ourselves, but remembered in time that we were marketeers, not underwriters. We were better off paying professional underwriters to do what *they* were good at, which was managing what turned out to be relatively low levels of risk.

Once Anglian had signed and made a success of our product, we gradually picked off the whole country: Thames, Severn Trent, Southern, Northumbrian, Yorkshire . . . Selling our warranties under the water company's name seemed only sensible to us at the time, but as we made deals with more and more companies, this strategy began to pay dividends. Any water company who decided they could do our job themselves was of course perfectly entitled to show us the door – only we would then be walking away with all their customers who had signed up, because one of the cleverest parts of the model was that we had customer ownership.

One or two companies resisted and said they'd come up with their own offering. Fair enough – but of course they generally weren't very good at it. This just wasn't their core business, whereas for us this was all we did, all we thought about, all day long.

Some HomeServe copies did better than others, but we outcompeted them all in the end, not least because we were (except in Sutton Water's area) the first to market. I talk a lot about second-mover advantage, and that's certainly a thing, but in this case being first to market meant we got the best, most loyal customers.

I say we trounced the competition; there was one exception. The one serious player who went for our business in a major way was British Gas. They had the resources and the know-how and they cross-sold their policy to all their customers. We returned the favour by trying to crack the gas market, but gas was a lot harder because, of course, British Gas had all the engineers.

Gas had been a public utility for years and years, and back then 'the man from the Gas Board' was the authority, the only person you could call on in an emergency. This gave British Gas an armour that, no matter how tarnished its reputation became, protected them from all comers.

We kept looking at their operation and asking ourselves, 'How can we do that? How do we get a piece of that?' It's a healthy attitude, but we underestimated the power that comes from being a brand leader. British Gas had all the advantages of scale. They could slap just £2 a month on your gas bill and cover the repair of your boiler. It might not be the best job in the world – the consumer journalist and campaigner Esther Rantzen practically built her TV career on stories about British Gas – but they were the easiest option, and if you had to call them out every three months because the engineer wasn't getting to the root of your problem, well, they could swallow the cost of those repeated call-outs without blinking.

When you have that much of the market sewn up, doing a barely adequate job is enough. Depressing, even maddening, but true.

NEVER DODGE A THREAT

In business, you need to be dogged in pursuit of your values. This, however, does not mean that you should keep hammering away, doing the thing that you've always excelled at. There are always multiple ways to reach your goal, and you may need to switch tactics in pursuit of your core strategy. Small and medium-sized companies especially have to be really good at learning how to do new things, to act swiftly as things change and to experiment with products and processes.

I'll finish this chapter with a story from 1997 – the year I got married and, coincidentally, a year that nearly destroyed HomeServe.

In May 1997, the Labour government finally lost patience with the UK water companies. Some of those privatised companies were generating enormous profits, even as their infrastructure decayed and the number of leaks from their pipes soared. The deputy prime minister at the time was John Prescott. He called their bosses in for a 'water summit' and – well, Prescott was a bit of a force of nature, and let's just say he made his displeasure known.

The very least these companies could do, he said, given the increasing shoddiness of their service, was to offer their customers free repairs on the pipework leading into their property. Fixing things up to the stopcock and then abandoning the customer to their fates just wasn't on. Well, good for John Prescott. My admiration for his stand was tempered, though, when I realised that HomeServe's core insurance product was about to be gazumped, for free, by every water supply company in the country.

We went straight to work, fashioning a new core product from the wreckage of the old. We prepared to write to our customers: 'Good news! This part of your policy is now covered for free by the water companies, so the £25 you're paying us now covers . . .' – well, what could we make it cover, exactly? We made a list. What did the government's new legislation *not* cover?

The water companies, meanwhile, had been put on the defensive, and never thought to see this disruption to their industry as an opportunity. Instead, they did everything they could to mitigate the problem. Let's cover our customers' repairs for just the statutory two metres! Let's lobby our way out of making good our repairs! At HomeServe we watched, with no little amazement, as the water companies successfully argued their way out of one business opportunity after another.

And where they retreated, we advanced. Were our existing £25 premiums enough to cover some household repairs? Yes. In fact our new 'gold standard' policy, which guaranteed customers a two-hour response time and up to £2,000 cover for repairs and reinstatement work, need cost only £20 a year, and over the next ten years we sold more than two million of these policies.

So, 1997 was a bad year for the water companies, and if we hadn't pivoted and adapted, it would have seen the end of HomeServe. But we believe in copying and pivoting, and that out of every problem there comes an even bigger opportunity. That's how, thanks to John Prescott, 1997 ushered in our fastest ever period of growth.

SUMMING UP

Embrace your second-mover advantage

Don't waste your time reinventing the wheel. By adapting someone else's good idea, you can turn it into a brand new offering. HomeServe's world-beating market proposition grew out of early efforts to make 'man in a van' operations affordable, efficient and worthwhile. We didn't turn that aspiration into a world-beating brand by waiting around for inspiration. We got there by buying some vans and by making what felt like every conceivable mistake in operating them.

You can bet the farm that your best competitors are even now adapting your offering to create their own unique products and services. This is how markets grow and mature. That's why, as an entrepreneur, it's as important to educate yourself about your market as it is to innovate in it.

Stay open and learn

Business rewards curiosity, openness and a willingness to be useful. Your first idea is almost certainly not going to be your best idea. I have never been wildly interested in earrings, but I was very interested when I saw how I could pivot my little fly-tying business to serve an untapped need in the fashion market.

Learn from competitors. Befriend them and consult them and chip in with advice when they ask for it. It's no skin off your nose. Emulate what works well. Above all, pay attention! Be observant, and listen to what people are telling you.

Copy and adapt

Copying is not bad. It's essential for learning and growth. Magazine publishing is a great example of a 'copy-and-pivot business', as my experiences with *Business Leader* have confirmed; we're constantly learning from the feedback our content generates. For a more mainstream example, look no further than the low-cost gym chain Synergym in Spain – a copy of PureGym, which was itself a copy of a German low-cost gym chain. I have invested my own money in Synergym, expanding them from thirteen locations in 2019 to 107 today. We're on track to have two hundred gyms by 2027, fuelled by a desire to encourage more active lifestyles in an affordable way.

Mistakes are fuel

As HomeServe's early struggles all too eloquently demonstrate, the best ideas often come from mistakes. Keep your eyes open and ears pricked to turn setbacks into opportunities. Continuous improvement is key. Don't expect growth on its own to solve your problems, and however successful you become accept that the journey of improvement is never truly over.

Chapter Two

Find an Investor

As introduced in the previous chapter, Simon Blunt is the founder of the Mortgage Advice Bureau and, more recently, the House Buyer Bureau. Now that I've established him as a serious business figure, it's time for me to explain how Simon, Jeremy Middleton and I first met.

It began soberly enough: Simon and I had run into each other at the National Franchise Show, where he was exploring franchise opportunities in the mortgage market. We thought we might have business to do together, and Simon came up to my mortgage shop in Middlesbrough to talk it through. The franchising idea didn't work out, but then, a little later, I invited him up to Newcastle to meet Jeremy.

Over to Simon: 'The pair wanted someone to invest in their businesses, and I went and had a look at all of them. Though I had to admire their energy, nothing stood out to me as something I was desperate to invest in. And so, at the end of a long day, and an even longer evening (the pair were determined to be hospitable – "Have another drink, Simon!"), I said, "I'll lend you some money instead." I lent them £15,000 at 20 per cent interest, which was the unsecured bank borrowing rate at the time.

'I fell asleep on the train on the way back – they'd got me very drunk – and woke up with a start, trying to work out where I was. I had a vague memory of doing something completely stupid. I pulled the chequebook out of my suit pocket and looked at the stub, and it said, "£15,000, Middleton and Harpin".

'In those days, you could cancel a cheque, so as soon as I got back I went to see my cousin Richard, a venture capitalist with British investment company 3i. He'd run into Richard Harpin before. "Should I cancel the cheque?"'

'My cousin laughed like a drain: "You know what? Either that guy Harpin will be the next Richard Branson, or he'll be on the street."

'About a year later, I was on Hagley Road in Birmingham when I saw Richard clambering out of a rather nice car. He'd already paid me back, with interest. I went over to say hello and admire his new vehicle. Over a meal at the local TGI Friday's, I said, "You know, I thought it was fifty-fifty I'd ever get that money back."

'Richard choked back a laugh: "More like a million-to-one shot," he said. Then he got distracted, offered our waitress a job in his new call centre, got distracted again and walked out without paying the bill.

'I found out later that, prior to our evening out, bailiffs had been knocking at his door – only, due to a mix-up, they had gone to the wrong address and had ended up doorstepping Jeremy's wife by mistake. (I wish I'd been a fly on the wall for that one.) Some of the money I had lent the pair had gone to repay Richard's mother the money he had borrowed off her. With the rest of it, and by maxing out their credit cards, Richard and Jeremy had managed to keep the business going – and going pretty well.'

It's true: in those early days, before we struck a deal with (or even knew about) South Staffs, Jeremy and I were in all sorts of trouble, and not just with my mother. Our cash flow was so abysmal we had had to do a deal with the VAT people; they said they'd defer what we owed for that quarter until the new year, but some bright spark still contrived to send a bailiff round (at Christmas time, naturally) to try to seize Jeremy's wife's furniture.

Something had to be done. We'd each maxed out our credit cards to the tune of £10,000 apiece, and I'd managed to borrow £10,000 from my mother only on condition we never told Dad. Jeremy and I still dine out on the story of how we got Simon Blunt drunk enough to lend us £15,000, but actually the joke could well have been on us: you see, that was our *second* offer. Our first offer (which Simon declined) was 10 per cent of our business. With hindsight you can say Simon should have taken us up on the offer. He'd have been tens of millions of pounds better off if he had.

Back in the real world, though, and without the benefit of time travel, you can see how, when Simon turned down our then worthless share offer, Jeremy and I unwittingly dodged a huge bullet. We might have handed over 10 per cent of our future wealth, then and there, for a mere £15,000!

A little while later, and we made the same mistake *again*. Once more we were strapped for cash, in a big way. We offered fully half of our business to South Staffs for £100,000 and a three-legged table. Again, and more by luck than good management, we fell on our feet: South Staffs proved a friendly and supportive investor. They were also canny dealmakers. They made sure, when we signed, that they had options to increase their ownership, first to 62.5 per cent and then to 75 per cent at a low (four times) price/earnings ratio – options they exercised as soon as ever they could.

Why am I telling you this story? What's the moral here?

Well, the first and most obvious lesson is, don't sell yourself short, and don't wait until you're desperate for cash to go looking for an investor. Waiting until you're on the back foot to strike a deal is never a good idea.

Touker Suleyman puts this very neatly: 'If I were starting a business from scratch today,' he says, 'I would delay the search for investment for as long as I could. Many entrepreneurs give away too much, far too soon. If you haemorrhage your position early on, what have you got left to trade? You'll need still bigger investments later on, and you can end up with very little you can call your own. I would say, always prove the concept. Get the turnover up to a level where you're not making excuses or promising that next year will be miraculously better than this one. Prove what you can do, so you can put a real valuation on it.'

We talked about how, as investors, we valued the businesses we were interested in, and we very quickly discovered we shared a not-so-mild prejudice against tech start-ups, and for the same reason: their founders live for the most part in cloud cuckoo land. Very talented young people who understand technology impress me, but I worry that, with all that technical expertise, they neglect the fundamentals of business. They assume that they can raise money quite easily, and investors indulge them with valuations I can't make sense of at all. On what rational basis can you value a company at twenty times its current revenue?

'A lot of tech companies are now finding it very difficult to raise money,' Touker points out. 'I don't see that as a huge problem, to be honest. I see that as a chance to learn how to grow a business. When I started, I struggled to raise any money at all, so from my perspective, the last couple of years have simply seen us return to normal.'

This conversation reminded me of something Jeremy Middleton said when I asked him about his own current investment strategy. 'The one kind of business I won't touch,' he told me, 'is the one that's digging itself slowly into debt because of the staggering upturn that's just around the corner. I don't want to do hockey sticks for the simple reason I don't believe them. "We haven't done very well up to now, but we're going to do fantastically well!" Well, the answer to that is: do it, or don't do it. You're the visionary here, not me – it's your job to prove your business model.'

The second moral we can take from the story of our desperate and dangerous early investment 'strategy' is rather more subtle, but just as important.

By the time we demerged from South Staffs Water, Jeremy and I owned only a quarter of our company. The rest belonged to South Staffs. Now, how do you think we felt about that? The answer is, *we felt fine.*

While we might occasionally sigh over what might have been, and measure with broad gestures 'the one that got away', the fact is South Staffs bankrolled our success. We were building something extraordinary with South Staffs's money, so why ever would we resent the arrangement that made it possible in the first place?

Outside the business world, people assume that whoever owns the majority stake in a company acquires some sort of magical power – rights over the minority stakeholder's firstborn or whatever. TV programmes like *Dragons' Den* encourage this – witness all those arguments the dragons and their wards get into over who gets 51 per cent of the nothing.

Reality is very different. Jeremy's family office quite often takes up to 75 per cent of the company it's investing in, and all works swimmingly well. 'With that security at my back, I've been able to invest more deeply,' Jeremy explains, 'and that's given the entrepreneur the means to do what they want to do. For them, 25 per cent is quite enough. They still run the business, and we will still exit together.'

Our own careers offer a pretty good demonstration of what Jeremy's getting at. South Staffs took 52 per cent of us when we struck our joint venture deal, which left us with 24 per cent each. Because we were in a terrible negotiating position, because we were tiny and they were very big, they negotiated the right to purchase half of us again, which took us each down to 12 per cent. And you can see, just from the title of this book, what, by holding on to my stake, I've made out of *that*.

And Jeremy? Later, South Staffs offered to buy a further 6 per cent, and offered to buy him out. This was the first time he'd taken a payout, and was he weeping into his beer? 'Hardly. I'd been living on next to nothing, and all of sudden here was £5 million in my bank account. I was overjoyed at the time and I've never regretted it since. I thought to myself, "This lets me be free; this lets me do whatever I want." And I was right.'

Over the years Jeremy has been selling down his stake in HomeServe because he wanted to do his own thing. 'I don't worry about "the money I could have had" because I'm a human being, not a bank account. I've had the huge good fortune to be able to find the money I wanted, when I wanted it, to do with it what I wanted to do. At every stage of that process, I felt just as motivated. And one thing I'm sure of: ending up with a little of a lot is a heck of a lot more lucrative than hanging on to a lot of a little.'

DESPERATION IS NOT A GOOD LOOK

Let's start, then, from two principles. First, don't go looking for an investor when you're in a financial mess. Second, if you can establish a real and positive collaboration with your investor, then you can afford to think strategically about what stake you want to retain in your company.

Jeremy and I did everything backwards. We waited until we were broke to go looking for money, and we handed over way too much of our company too early on to people we didn't know very well. When you get into a pickle like that, it's very easy to become paranoid. Jeremy sees this all the time in his investment business. 'I'm always getting people who come up and say, "I've got a great business idea, but I can't tell you because you might do it." Okay, then I'm not going to invest in you, am I? And neither will anyone else.

'Then there are those who say, "I've got a business idea." What they mean is, "I've got an idea." It'll probably be a good idea, but unless and until you rub it up against the real world, you'll have no idea whether or not it's going to be one of that vanishingly small fraction that works as a business.'

Everyone has their own way of going about things, of course, but I've noticed that Jeremy is always extremely open about everything in relation to any of the businesses that he's involved in. 'I'm trying to form a long-term relationship here, so misrepresenting anything would be a disaster,' he explains. 'In fact, I don't try to sell anybody anything: I'm just trying to find a mutual match.'

We can think of investment as coming in four stages, and we may as well use HomeServe's journey to illustrate them. Stage one: In the very early FastFix days, investment came from friends and family and the little bit of trade we could drum up. Stage two: South Staffs Water provided us with early-stage growth capital in 1993, when it invested £100,000 for half our business. Stage three: In 2004, listing on the stock exchange enabled HomeServe to raise its profile and create a unique identity. Stage four: Finally, Brookfield, the private equity investor, acquired us at the start of 2023 and helped us focus on long-term growth and a new strategy of owning home infrastructure. (Of course, the last two stages here are to some degree interchangeable. Whether companies float or sell to private equity, and when, depends very much on their particular circumstances.)

At each stage, our financial reporting became more robust, until we were preparing monthly board reports for our directors. For those at the start of their growth journey, this might sound arduous, but there comes a point where the discipline of preparing regular reviews is a real help, and the main method for spotting opportunities for growth and issues that need immediate attention.

Let's take a close look at that crucial first round of investments. Why are you looking for money in the first place? Strange as this sounds, your first investments should not be about expanding your business – or at least, that shouldn't be your first priority. Those crucial early investments are about taking the pressure off and de-risking your life so that you're not spending all your creative time wondering where the next mortgage payment will come from. A bit of seed capital also means you don't have to worry about profits temporarily going into reverse when you hire additional staff, or open retail stores. Third, investment should bring expertise from your financial partner, such as coaching, mentoring and decades of advice forged at the sharp end of your chosen industry.

When you should do this is a little trickier – and here's where I went wrong all those years ago, giving away far too much equity in my desperation to keep the business afloat. I should have got my business model working before looking to raise external investment. I should have kept HomeServe smaller until we had perfected our approach with our own finances, instead of giving away so much of the business.

Early investments are about giving someone else skin in your game. True, there are few greater sources of motivation than that. But you need to find someone who can help you with knowledge, expertise and experience – not just money. Potential investors should be judged on all those criteria. An investor has to fit the culture of your business.

Listen to your gut. (The gut is the product, so I've read, of fifteen million years of evolution, and this might explain why it is rarely wrong.) Don't listen to blarney – and don't sell yourself short.

There are all kinds of investors to choose from (don't forget your family), and surprisingly few clear dos and don'ts. Seeking investment is much less about finance than you expect, and far, far more to do with psychology. What you're after is someone who gets your business enough to invest in it in the long term, but not so much that they end up wanting to run it for you.

As an entrepreneur turned investor in other entrepreneurs, I was startled to discover that Simon Arora – who grew the discount retailer B&M from a £500,000 acquisition into a £5 billion empire – didn't think entrepreneurs were much good as investors. I'll grit my teeth and let him speak because his point's a good one: 'One of the features of entrepreneurs is they tend to be control freaks, so there's always the risk, particularly if they get involved at the start-up stage, that they won't be able to resist trying to run things. For myself, I could certainly see a situation where I end up getting sucked into running something – and I certainly don't want to be running a business five, six, seven days a week any more!

'And of course from the founder's point of view this sort of thing can be pretty ruinous. It's never a good idea to have two cooks in the same kitchen. That's why, for myself, I'd be more comfortable investing as a shareholder in a medium-sized business, where there's an established management team and a proven business model.'

When investment deals go wrong, the horror stories tend to linger, and this has made the business of finding an investor appear far more dangerous and shark-infested than it really is. Once in a blue moon, dreadful things happen. Look up Southern Cross care homes and Debenhams department stores for high-profile examples of how debt-happy, asset-stripping private-equity (PE) opportunists can take down your life's work with their irresponsible investments.

But they're easily outnumbered by inspiring PE stories that never make the headlines, where the prospects of undervalued and underperforming companies have been transformed, and produced exceptional returns for their investors.

The cardinal rule is: never go into a negotiation unless you have a clear blueprint for what you want to achieve. Private equity companies go for growth; are you ready for that? They'll insist (rightly) that you can grow fastest by doing just one thing; has your business matured enough that it knows what that one thing is? The best PE houses are very good indeed at spotting opportunities, and ruthless about clearing away clashing priorities and fractious personalities; is your team strong and supportive enough to take the medicine?

In 2012, the private equity firm CD&R bought a majority stake in B&M, and Sir Terry Leahy, the former boss of Tesco, became chairman. Though the arrangement was short-lived, and two years later B&M was floated on the stock market (where it achieved a valuation of £2.7 billion), B&M's founder Simon Arora has no regrets: 'CD&R brought lots to our table in those two years. They came in around the time that we started making inroads in Europe, but we had no experience at all of mergers and acquisitions, and CD&R helped with the whole process. There was a lot to think about in negotiating a transaction in an overseas territory where the legal system is different, the language trips you up every five minutes, and even the different accounting styles between territories can throw you for a loop. Selling the majority stake to CD&R also brought the family some financial security; it matters to me that the next generation won't have to worry about keeping a roof over their head.'

PE boards work closely with your executive team to create a new roadmap or blueprint; one you'll implement together. If the organisation is subsequently resized, savings will be reinvested in a more focused operation. Public companies love to talk about 'purpose', but in my experience, those backed by private equity are far more adept at providing teams with purpose, with everyone focused on making the company the best it can be.

I can't tell you how often the chief executive of some public company has quietly confessed to me that the endless box-ticking demands of the stock market have got in the way of their plans.

Governance challenges, audit and remuneration committees, corporate social responsibility considerations – yes, they're important, but in having to juggle all of them all at once according to some feckless industry-standard timetable, growth suffers.

This is what private equity does: it frees leadership teams to focus on what they should focus on in the moment. The other thing to remember about private equity is that there are as many ways of investing as there are investors. At one extreme, there are investors who want blisteringly fast growth and are prepared to dig deep to buy their way into it. Naturally, once they've done this, they'll expect you to sell the moment you hit the top of your company's market valuation.

At the other end of the spectrum, there's Jeremy Middleton, whose private office, Middleton Enterprises, looks for long-term opportunities. Significantly, he refuses to use the words 'private equity'. 'We're calling it a family office,' he explains, 'not a PE vehicle or a fund, because we want to highlight the fact that we're only interested in making long-term, even lifetime investments.'

Middleton Enterprises is not too different from my own investment company, Growth Partner, and Jeremy and I have endless fun arguing over who's been copying whom. The boring truth, however, is that Jeremy and I shared many experiences, drew the same conclusions and built different businesses off the back of them. Jeremy's looking at companies that are at least breaking even and at most are making around £2 million profit. I step in at a later stage. Jeremy will put in one or two million in the first round; I put in much more. Jeremy's looking to end up with a stake of around £5 million, while I go higher, in pursuit of bigger growth numbers. Jeremy's more conservative, perhaps because he's been investing a lot longer than I have – but I've built the bigger beast.

Jeremy's inspiration came from when a business of his that was well covered, and making a couple of million in profit, needed some short-term finance. No clearing bank would make him a serious offer: 'Some said, "Come back when you're making £5 million." Well, by then it's hardly an early-stage business, is it? In the end we had to go to alternative lenders who charge 7.5 or 8 per cent over the base interest rate.'

This, anyway, was the experience of one good, profitable business; a sad story but one that Jeremy was inclined to write off to bad luck. He was horrified to discover that the problem is systemic. 'The lack of easy finance is forcing the founders of small and medium-sized enterprises to sell equity in their businesses long before they should need to,' Jeremy says. 'Most people in the venture capital business aren't interested in good, solid, ordinary compounding businesses. The worst of them just want to invest £5 million and hothouse the company into a premature sale. So there's a huge shortage of capital for companies scaling up.'

Jeremy takes a lot of pride in running a business that understands entrepreneurs and their needs. 'Founders may have worked for ten years without earning any real money,' he points out. 'Their peers, meanwhile, are all lawyers and CFOs and goodness knows what, and they're all living very well. So, we're open to buying some extra equity if that's what it'll take to re-energise an exhausted founder. The best result for the company and the employees is for the company to compound over the long haul, and that means the founder should stay.'

I'm very much of the same mind. Our approach here comes as a surprise to some entrepreneurs, though. They think, when they're raising money, 'For my investors' sake, I'd better think about selling.' To which the obvious reply is, 'Why?' The money you'd get from the sale is money you've got anyway – it's just tied up in the business. Now, if you want to release some of that money, that's fine, though my advice, and Jeremy's, and Touker's, and most everyone's, would be to hold on as long as possible, because then you'll get a larger return.

But why ever would you want to sell? Jeremy has found that there are a couple of reasons, both of them dumb. 'One, you think you want to go and lie on a beach. Believe me, you don't. You'll be bored out of your skull. Two, you want to do another business. Well, let's say you succeed; that business is almost certainly going to turn out looking very similar to the one you're in now. "So why do you want to sell?" I ask them. "Well," comes the reply, "I've worked so hard, and it's a real pain doing this bit and that bit . . ." '

Now, this is absolutely *not* a reason to sell the business. Rather, it's your wake-up call, telling you to shed the bits of the job you don't like doing and get out of the way of people who do like doing them. Hire your replacement, and go and do what you're best at. You love strategy? Then be strategy director. Or be chair, or a non-exec, or just a straight shareholder. But don't sell out! As your investor, why would I want you to sell? If the company's working, I'm making money. And if it's not working, well, we're probably not going to be able to sell it anyway.

For any serious investor, predictability is key, and that's why the most dependable investors congregate around the most dependable businesses. When you begin investing you quickly discover (or ought to – my own early experiments were nothing to write home about) that the easiest businesses to predict are those that have a repeatable model. If you have a retail company that's managed to open five stores, then it's a fair bet that with your help, they can work out how to open another five, and then another five. Retail is a good investment because it's relatively predictable. A company doing B2B sales is a more difficult proposition. Someone might say, 'Business is great: I've sold a lot of these products in the last month!' but neither you nor they know, with any certainty, whether they'll sell a lot next month, or be paid the same amount.

Some would say the most predictable business models are B2B SaaS (software as a service) businesses. 'I've invested in them in the past,' Jeremy concedes, 'but their valuations are far too high. I'm only really interested in buying businesses that are valued as a multiple of the cash they generate. That is, real businesses at real prices.'

No matter how confident you might feel in your idea, approach or business model, stay small until you have truly found what works.

STOP THINKING ABOUT MONEY

Remember FastFix, a business that had no cost-effective way of meeting the demand it generated? Instead of a growing profitable business, Jeremy and I ended up creating a growing *loss-making* business. No good investor will invest in you in that state (Simon Blunt didn't).

Growth, remember – and take this from someone who loves growth – is a horrible index of success. Anyone can grow by getting into debt, and anyone can fuel this growth by making a staggeringly unwise investment.

What you need from an investor, at the bare minimum, is someone who understands risk. 'I manage risk by working my way backwards,' explains Touker Suleyman. 'What's the worst-case scenario? If I'm taking a risk that's going to send the whole ship to the bottom – well, I just wouldn't take that risk. I'd come up with an alternative and then, once again, I'd work out the worst that could happen. At a certain point the reward will be worth the risk. But if I want to be around tomorrow with a roof over my head, then I have to start by assessing the risk.'

One of the best things you can do as a founder looking for investment is to study the psychology of risk. It will help you sort good investors from bad, and give you an invaluable glimpse into the motives of your potential business partner.

There's a library's worth of books about risk out there, but few better introductions than *Risk Roulette: The Surprising Reasons Why Some Businesses Work and Others Fail* (2024), by Graham Ruddick, a veteran business journalist, now editor-in-chief of *Business Leader*. 'You can employ all the strategy you like,' Graham explains, 'but in the end, you're working with psychology.' One of Graham's big discoveries while he was working on his book was that the more risk-averse we are, the more easily we can be led astray! 'A person who's afraid to take risks is also afraid of missing out,' Graham explains, 'because that too is a risk.'

There's a brief part in the book where he mentions me as someone who, after a lifetime of entrepreneurial activity, has finally realised that he can't do everything. 'Part of it is growing older, and having the desire to protect what they have,' says Graham, 'but I think it's also that they've conquered their fear of missing out.'

No matter how much investors try to quantify what they do, in the end they're as much at the mercy of their own natures as the rest of us. Many investors swear by 'EV' – that's 'expected value', the average outcome you can expect from a particular decision. You work out how likely something is to succeed, then you multiply that fraction by the value you'll get if, by the grace of God, it does succeed. Good luck turning *that* into an objective calculation.

The poster child for this kind of thinking was – until he came quite spectacularly unstuck – Sam Bankman-Fried, who thought about everything in terms of expected value. Regrettably, he became obsessed with the gains people might make on the rare wins, and lost sight of the downside completely. He talked as if risking complete destruction was the only way to play. And that, famously, was the end of him, and the end of his FTX cryptocurrency exchange. It turned out that billions of dollars of customer funds were being used to cover his other losses.

'EV' thinking is especially prevalent among those daredevil types who invest in tech start-ups. Perhaps I ought to offer an olive branch to those readers developing wonderful new tech ideas. I'm not likely to invest in you, but there are those who will and, joking aside, they're not all buccaneers.

Here's Graham to explain: 'UK investors are constantly being criticised for not investing in promising tech companies. They're told, "Look over there! US investors are taking all these fearless risks! What's the matter with you?" But when you look into investor behaviour in the US, there's nothing fearless about it. I'd go so far as to say these US investment decisions are being driven by fear – the fear of missing out, the fear that somebody else will do what you're not doing and will make you look stupid. Not long ago, Babylon, the digital GP service, listed in the US, and its founder said at the time, "America is a great place to list. They get tech businesses. The UK is too risk-averse." Sure enough, US investors piled in, and sure enough the operation went bust. The US investors were taken to the cleaners and you had all these UK investors standing around winking at each other.

'But you know, this really isn't a story about wise and unwise investment. It's about different styles of investment. US investors simply think about risk in a different way. They set themselves up correctly to handle FOMO. That is, they're carefully designed to *lose*, 90 per cent of the time, on high-risk ventures. This then frees them up to capitalise on the 10 per cent of wild ideas that do pay off. The numbers make sense; they're just being used to play a game we're not very used to in the UK.

'And vice versa: UK funds are often criticised for being conservative, but again, they're set up correctly and doing well – you just have to know what game they're playing. Investors buy into UK funds on the understanding they will get a certain return. The funds have to deliver. A few points above base is success, real success. It's just different to the success a venture capital firm would pursue, which has raised money on the basis that most of its investments will fail, but one might be the next Apple or Amazon.'

WHAT DO INVESTORS WANT?

Now we've got the lie of the land, here is my own personal investment philosophy. My advice to small businesses is stay small and keep testing and pivoting until you find the winning model and it's profitable – without burning through lots of cash. When it's your own money, you value it more and are more sensible about how it's spent.

In terms of where to find capital, start with your own savings, or try to remortgage. Then seek out friends and family before heading to crowdfunding or venture capital, to get your model right. Private equity will be applicable once your business is generating a reasonable profit, while a stock exchange listing is an option when the business is bigger still.

For myself, I like the idea of a global business. I built one of my own, and I'm now investing in others that have global potential. At

Growth Partner, my investment business, we back only proven and profitable firms, not start-ups or early-stage non-profitable ones, and we prefer to work with entrepreneurs who are focused on getting their business model right before reaching for the cash. I've seen many crowdfunded and venture capital-funded businesses in which the founders ended up with a minority shareholding because, with the model still in flux, they hadn't negotiated from a position of strength. As a result, they diluted their ownership and diminished their incentive.

Today, Growth Partner looks to take minority stakes in medium-sized companies that have already hit upon a good business model – say, one that turns between £2 and £5 million in annual profit. I'm not interested in all that '51 per cent of nothing' carry-on. I'll happily settle for a healthy minority stake, while the company's founders continue to weave their magic – and while I'm about it, I'll make sure they're getting all the support they need. The point, for me – and the pleasure – is to collaborate, connect businesses and share ideas. We want to help medium-sized businesses step-change their own expansion, advising them on why and when to take capital, and from which sources.

There are 75,000 medium-sized companies out there in the UK (employing 15–250 staff and with sales of over £3 million a year), and Jeremy's dead right, nobody is really watching out for them. Imagine what would happen if we could get some of them to grow, doubling the number of large companies in this country. That's more than possible; as I mentioned in the Introduction, the UK has only 7,500 large companies and they employ 40 per cent of the working population – 10.6 million people! Imagine the enormous economic growth we could trigger, simply by scaling up our best medium-sized companies!

Why is the middle being forgotten? For small to medium-sized enterprises and start-ups, there is no better place than the UK to start a business. The tax rate is relatively low, and though we always complain about it, there's really not very much red tape to get through. But then a business, once it employs twenty or thirty people, is categorised as medium-sized, and it gets forgotten about. The country is great at start-ups, terrible at scale-ups.

With a £100 million war chest of my own money, and a team of eleven, Growth Partner is working with thirteen great entrepreneurs, and we hope to double that number over the coming years. We are investing in leaders, not just businesses – those with resilience, persistence and an ability to learn from their mistakes and put the ambitions of the business above their own personal aspirations.

We've met one of them already in this book: the haircare entrepreneur Victoria Lynch. Victoria started doing hair extensions for her family and friends in Stockton at the age of thirteen. Even as Growth Partner started taking an interest in Additional Lengths, her £5 million turnover business rocketed to over £4 million in annual profit, making her question whether she needed our cash at all.

Well, I don't suppose she did. What she did need was investment in the broader sense of that word – and Victoria's decision to say 'yes' to Growth Partner gives us a great opportunity to explore how the investment relationship works beyond the balance sheet.

'I'd reached a point where I knew I couldn't do everything myself' she recalls. 'Finding the right people is always crucial, especially in our location in the north-east, where the talent pool can be limited. I had somehow cobbled together a great team, but we were a small group punching above our weight, and sooner or later we were going to come unstuck. For a long time, it was just me and two other people running the show. We were a thin team doing incredibly demanding work. We moved mountains together, literally shifting inventory in the back of my car because our delivery van cancelled! If we were to keep growing, we needed more support, and I needed to get better at delegating responsibilities.

'I started my company very young and had had to learn everything on my own. I didn't have any mentors or coaches guiding me along the way. I wouldn't say I was just winging it, but I definitely had to figure things out as I went along. Like many business owners, I've worn many hats and I've had to handle every aspect of the business. I wasn't considering selling my business or taking on any external investment – I'd never needed it before – but I was looking for knowledge and support.'

Actually, Growth Partner found her, and contacted her accountants to ask if she would have a conversation with us. Victoria's business was one calculated to catch my eye: founder-led and profitable. 'My accountants suggested I take the meeting,' Victoria remembers, 'and even though I was initially reluctant, and usually steer clear of those conversations, Growth Partner saw potential in my business that I hadn't fully recognised. Hearing their perspective was eye-opening.'

We spent about nine months in discussions and there was a point where Victoria almost backed out: her company was growing at such a speed it no longer fitted our investment criteria! What sealed the deal was less the money (important as that was for Additional Lengths's expansion) than the community Growth Partner has built up among its founders. We're very much focused on the idea of partnership. We've created a family of entrepreneurs helping each other succeed. And because I've been in the trenches myself, I understand the dedication and sacrifice it takes to build a business. It's not just a job; it's about pouring your heart and soul into something. That shared experience is Growth Partner's unique selling point.

SUMMING UP

Investors will not save you (but they will accelerate your success!)
If I had to reduce this chapter to a single sound bite, it would be: 'Don't go after investors out of desperation.' I did, and survived the experience, but I can promise you that was very much more to do with luck than good management. Not everyone's lucky enough to run, at just the right moment, into a Simon Blunt or a South Staffs Water.

Investors are not there to save you. They are there to encourage you, enable you and open doors for you. If you can prove your business model before seeking investment, so much the better:

you can then concentrate on finding investors who really 'get' your business and its values.

Once you've got a business that works, however, don't be coy about your success. Go after money that will de-risk your domestic life and enable you to concentrate on your business. Everyone's afraid of investment mistakes. But the more thinking time you can obtain for yourself, the less likely those mistakes will be.

Investment is about collaboration

Early investments are about finding someone to work with, a partner who puts 'skin in the game' and shares knowledge and expertise. Initial investments enable you to dedicate time to develop the business; they're more than just a quick cash injection. South Staffs's support in kind, its phones and desks and IT support, were in those vital early days quite as valuable as its money.

Don't sell yourself short

Look for investors who can help you build a strong foundation for future growth. Simon Blunt knew us better than we knew ourselves, and we dodged a huge bullet when he declined our ridiculous and desperate offer to hand over 10 per cent of our future wealth for just £15,000. Even as a small business, don't undervalue your potential. Listen to your gut instinct. In the early days, your gut will often tell you more than any financial figures.

Chapter Three

Get Some Coachment

Leaders live or die by the quality of the counsel they receive. In business, that counsel takes one of three forms. First, there is the tactical advice you receive, day to day, from your trusted colleagues. Their eagle-eyed efforts will detect those shoals and rocks you may have missed. (The art of hiring people smarter than you are, and encouraging them to be as smart as possible, even to the point of being able to replace you, will be the subject of Chapter Five.)

The second form of advice you need is mentorship. Business mentors understand your sector. They can steer you around pitfalls, and they can open doors for you. Their advice isn't tactical. They won't (or shouldn't) try to run your business for you. Their advice is strategic, helping you chart your chosen course through choppy waters.

Business coaches offer you a third kind of support. They'll help you integrate and internalise the advice of others, and the lessons you're gathering from your own experience. They'll help you hold everything together in your own head, and at a level of detail that you can actually handle. They'll ensure that, in your pursuit of success, you hold to your values and manage your own life and happiness. They will help you weigh up options and make the right decision. What they *won't* do is offer advice.

The bulk of this chapter will be about the relatively formal business of coaching and mentoring. To set the scene, though, I want to run by you some of the responses I got when I asked some formidable people how they had acquired their business skills.

When I talked to him, Touker Suleyman had just delivered an Oxford Union speech. Someone asked him what list of principles or books or literature he follows. He could only reply, 'None. It's all just fifty years of experience. Read a lot of books, by all means,' he advises, 'but if at the same time you're not gaining experience, then those books are just going to get tangled up in your head. Whereas, if you've lived as long as I have, and experienced what I have, you could write a book yourself.'

Ben Francis is the founder of the sports apparel company Gymshark. Ben tips his cap to formal learning but reckons nothing beats experience. 'I remember when we opened our first store on Regent Street. We had done all our forecasting, pulling in everyone who knew about retail. A week before we opened, a chap who had spent his life in retail came to visit. I told him we planned to do ten million in revenue. He said, "What's your square footage?" I told him. "What's your average order value?" I told him. He said, "You won't do ten million—"

' "But we've done the numbers!"

' "You'll do fifteen," he said, and – twelve months later – we turned £15 million in revenue.'

A happy story indeed – but it's quite scary to discover how inadequate calculations and forecasts can be next to an opinion informed by years of actual experience.

When I started, I felt very much like Touker: experience is king, therefore experience is enough. Seeking advice was not the natural instinct that it has since become. I've come to realise that there's a certain amount of luck involved in getting the right experience. We should de-risk that process as much as we can. I'm convinced my businesses would have grown faster, and I would have made fewer mistakes, if I had asked for advice from the right people.

Too often, in my early days, and seduced by my own self-confidence, I made up my mind before meeting a board I was worried might block me. I discovered the value of mentorship only slowly, and by degrees. Now and again, I would meet people who were more experienced and successful than me, and I'd try to learn from these encounters. Sir John Peace made a big impression on me, I remember. He led the credit-checking and data business in Nottingham that came out of Great Universal Stores and later became Experian. Then there was Brian Whitty, the CEO of South Staffordshire Group in the early days of HomeServe, and HomeServe chairman when we demerged in 2004. For twelve years he served as my sounding board, mentor and chief challenger of my dafter ideas. And I had role models, of course, such as Sir Richard Branson and Lord (Alan) Sugar, and I would watch their careers, read their books and follow their stories.

Otherwise, the nearest I ever came to having a mentor was filling my bookshelves full of biographies and business books, histories and what the bookshops call (a bit pretentiously) 'smart thinking'. I was sixteen years into my HomeServe journey before the penny dropped and I finally took positive action to get exactly the advice and guidance I needed.

The thing about wisdom is that you must be bullish in its pursuit. (There's a reason why, in those martial arts movies, the pupil has to go through hell and high water to get the adept's attention.) In 2010, I decided HomeServe's US expansion needed to accelerate. I couldn't see what we were doing that was holding us back, and neither could my colleagues. I decided to seek advice. Flicking through the *Sunday Times* Rich List, my eyes were drawn to Nigel Morris, a Brit who'd lived in Washington, DC, for eighteen years and had made it big with his Capital One credit card business.

I sent him emails. Nothing. I sent him handwritten letters. Nothing. I dispatched him a package through DHL – and got no response. I started calling his office. One evening, Nigel himself answered: 'I recognise your name,' he said. 'Sorry I've not got back to you, but next time you're in Washington, look me up and I'll give you an hour.' 'Funnily enough,' I lied, 'I'm there tomorrow. Can I pop by then?' Thank goodness there was still a plane ticket available: first thing the next morning, I was on the first flight out of Heathrow. By 2 p.m., I was sitting in Nigel's office. (The thing about 'no' in business is that it usually means something like 'not yet', or 'not if you put it like that'. It's not an absolute. It's the default answer given by people whose time is valuable – and whose isn't? – a gate to open, not an unclimbable wall.)

Three hours later, my head spinning from what would turn out to be the first of a few sessions, I came out of Nigel's office knowing roughly what was wrong with HomeServe USA and, roughly, what we could do to fix it. First, we were based in Miami (and at the end of a busy runway, too – but that's another story). Miami's great for a holiday, but it's not a place (or wasn't, in those days) to run a US business. We needed to relocate to the country's more business-minded northeast. Second, we needed a US-born CEO. Jonathan King (a pivotal figure in HomeServe – we'll hear a lot more from him in the coming pages) had done a superb job as managing director, responsible for establishing and developing our US operation. For all that, now that our expansion depended on signing up the very largest US utilities, we needed our business culture to reflect the national culture at the very highest level.

Putting Nigel Morris's advice into action transformed us. At the time of our meeting, seven years into our US operation, the business was turning a $10 million annual profit. Following the meeting, and before he handed over to an American CEO, Jonathan oversaw our transformational move from Florida to Connecticut. Fourteen years later we were making $240 million a year.

Nigel didn't tell me what to do. His experience helped me understand what to do. He prodded and probed, listened and analysed, empathised and argued. Now, that's a mentor – someone who helps to show rather than demands to tell.

I had learned my lesson, and from then on I searched out people who could advise me on my most important strategic decisions. When HomeServe bought Checkatrade in 2017, we needed to expand the business rapidly, and that involved a crash course in understanding digital marketplaces. I managed to get Jeff Boyd, who was the chief executive and then chairman of Booking.com, to meet with me and help. I also sought advice from Steve Kaufer, the co-founder of TripAdvisor, and Scott Forbes, an American who was chairman of Rightmove in the UK. All three of them were incredibly generous with their time and insight, and within weeks of us meeting and chatting through Checkatrade's issues, we had started to transform the business.

LEARN FROM THE BEST

One of the first questions I ask anyone I'm interviewing for a job is also one of the most revealing: 'How do you prefer to learn? Do you read business books, and if so, which is your favourite, and why?' I want to work with people who are curious about the lives and experiences of others, who want to understand how visionaries achieved success, and how to avoid their mistakes. There is always something new to learn, and with an estimated 15,000 business books published every year in the UK alone, there's plenty of choice.

In 2003, I came across *Good to Great* (2001), a bestseller by the management expert Jim Collins. Rather than just promoting his important opinions, *Good to Great* showed Collins rolling up his sleeves and getting stuck into analysing the operations of a staggering 1,435 companies. From those companies, all successful in their field, he identified eleven – like Wells Fargo and Kimberly-Clark – that were performing exceptionally well.

Were these companies simply on a lucky streak? (After all, someone has to come top of a list.) Or were there underlying principles that, if followed, allowed any company to make the transition from good to great? Jim reckoned there were twelve such principles that, if followed, could tip a company towards greatness. Nothing ventured, nothing gained: some years later, in 2019, I emailed Jim, told him about HomeServe and got a couple of invitations to his annual CEO seminar in Boulder, Colorado.

Tom Rusin, the new (American!) CEO of HomeServe USA, came with me, but he was sceptical. 'The book's great,' he agreed, 'but Jim's never run a business. How's this guy who's never had to be down in the weeds, fighting the battles, dealing on a day-to-day basis with all those things that can go wrong, going to tell us how to run a business?'

Fair enough – but I had a bet with myself that this wouldn't be Jim's way of doing things. Jim wasn't going to tell us how to run our companies. He wasn't going to second-guess us. He was going to give us some bigger picture that – 'down in the weeds' as we were – we couldn't glimpse for ourselves. He was going to give us a unique, and uniquely valuable, perspective on our work.

Tom and I found ourselves in a room full of successful, high-achieving CEOs and founders sharing their ideas about how Jim's principles related to their own businesses. The atmosphere was electric. More than that, it was honest. Even American CEOs were publicly recalling some of the mistakes they had made along the way! I remember sitting next to one chap, Jack, an Australian food services billionaire in his seventies – still curious, still devoted to learning – who then and there revealed to me one of the secrets I discuss in this book: 'We're foxes,' he told me. 'Always hunting around for the next opportunity. And I'm beginning to think we should be hedgehogs, massively defended against distraction.' Chapter Eight, 'Follow a *not*-to-do list', is for Jack.

Tom later confessed to being so impressed by Jim's school of thinking that he finally 'got religion'. He remembers, 'In one of the breakouts I said to Richard, "If we are going to do this, we have to really commit. It can't be something we do and then six months later we are switching to something else."'

I agreed. We needed to choose our framework of values wisely, and then we had to be prepared to commit to it fully. We doubled down on those values Jim Collins identified as key to excellence in business. There's no point navigating if you can't steer, so we agreed that, before we ever agonised over the direction of the company, we would focus on hiring the right people. We adopted, without hesitation, Jim's definition of an excellent leader (what he calls a 'Level 5'): someone who combines professional will with personal humility. We also wrote up our own 'hedgehog strategy', which we'll discuss at greater length in Chapter Eight.

That was half the work. The other half was learning to look at our company as an outsider might look at it, and learning how to abstract clear, useful lessons from a complex enterprise. It was never going to be enough for us to parrot Jim Collins. We had to learn how to be our own Jim Collins.

Out of that experience emerged something we called 'The HomeServe Academy' – an online learning resource that brought together the knowledge, skills and behaviours that make up HomeServe's leadership DNA. At the same time, and in each of our territories, we rolled out what was effectively our business bible: *Good to Great: The HomeServe Way*.

INSPIRE BREAKTHROUGH

One day in 2015, at around 2 a.m., I woke suddenly, my brow moist with sweat, my heart pounding. I'm normally a sound sleeper, but on this occasion I woke up gripped by fear. 2015 was a very good year. I had by that point spent over two decades building, running and growing HomeServe, and I couldn't have been happier about its success or prouder of my team's achievements. And yet I was in turmoil. What if I suddenly stopped enjoying running HomeServe? I would go from working flat out to leaving and doing nothing and feeling unfulfilled for the rest of my days.

In footballing terms, I fretted that, having scored a hat trick in the first half, I might not even touch the ball in the second. I needed a break so that I could find space to think about what I might do next. With support from my chairman, I enrolled on a four-day authentic leadership development course at Harvard Business School, to 'become the type of leader you most admire'.

It was an intense experience in which I had to outline exactly what I wanted from life. It forced me to ask questions of myself and, while everyone around me wrote down pages of material, all I could come up with was two words (which may not surprise friends who say I can be slow on the uptake). But those two words re-energised me and have shaped my working life since. They've given me a purpose that I always felt was inside me but couldn't quite articulate. They were: 'inspire breakthrough'.

Since that Boston trip, I've found time outside my day job to help those who want to learn how to accelerate growth in their business and avoid the mistakes I've made. All it took was two words, but inspiring their breakthroughs has given me new purpose. Just as I had approached Capital One founder Nigel Morris for advice, so people had been coming to me, effectively asking me to mentor them. Having benefited so much myself from others' advice, I was more than happy to give back. I felt a sense of obligation – also, to be quite frank, I enjoyed it.

But I was sharply aware that war stories, while entertaining, are not real advice. By then I had over thirty years of business experience to share, but unless I knew what each entrepreneur and CEO wanted out of life and out of their business, how could any of that help them? War stories are fun, but I actually wanted to be of use.

I recognised that if I wanted to offer people real value, I should do some study and get some training. And so, in 2023, I earned my papers as a business coach through INSEAD (the Institut Européen d'Administration des Affaires), a non-profit graduate business school. Along with online coaching, learning, assignments and assessments, the course involved spending twelve days at its campus in Fontainebleau in France. There were thirty-six of us in the class, and we were an interesting lot. Some in the group had a vocation to teach and mentor, and this was to be their first, and possibly sole, career. Others were business executives trying to bring real substance to their new, non-executive roles. Others were here out of pure curiosity, believing the course would enrich their business experience.

The idea of business coaching is relatively new. It began in the 1940s but didn't come into its own until the 1980s. The point of coaching is to get the client to ask the best questions they can of themselves and their business: to establish goals, examine realities, consider options and encourage action. When I first went to INSEAD, I didn't even really know the difference between coaching and mentoring. Now I understand that mentoring uses experience and shares learning, while coaching facilitates thinking, exploring options and decision-making. I've learned that how I advise people is just as important as what advice I give. I set out choices, rather than forcing an opinion. 'Why do you think that?' 'What are you trying to achieve?' 'What choices do you have here?' Sometimes the most basic questions elicit the most powerful solutions.

LEARN TO LISTEN

Thinking about my own business experience, I realised that coaching alone would never have been especially useful or satisfying for me; that the magic formula involved a coaching session combined with mentoring. Had I tried something like that before my INSEAD training, I suspect the result would have been a bit of a mishmash. Now I have the tools to build something with some structure to it.

I've badged it 'Coachment', and it's something I make available to my Growth Partner businesses. This is where a coaching session, used to diagnose issues, is immediately followed by a mentoring session, which applies business experience and knowledge to those issues. Using a medical analogy, coaching is a diagnostic process; mentorship is like a consultation, in which the diagnosis and its implications are explored.

I might be coaching one or two people at any given time, and one or two sessions usually suffice. Every person and every business is different, but some general themes emerge. The leader's besetting difficulty is (surprise, surprise) leadership. How do you handle bright, often very likeable people in an environment that may make them vital to your business one day and redundant or even harmful to it the next? In one recent session I had the co-founder of a business come to the painful conclusion that they had selected the wrong person to be their CEO, and had let go of the reins of their company too soon. I'm very sympathetic to situations like this because I know what strength I've drawn from having colleagues who've stayed the course at HomeServe for twenty years or more. Every time things don't pan out that way, it's a wrench and a loss.

Another besetting problem I encounter was demonstrated, somewhat comically, the other day by a *Business Leader* member who turned up to our first session with their prepared questions closely printed across three A4 sheets. With that lot ahead of us, I hardly needed to open my mouth before the problem revealed itself. In a small voice, the member said, 'I'm doing too much, aren't I?' Needless to say, our session focused on the value of focus and the *not*-to-do list (see Chapter Eight).

I think if I had trained as a coach earlier in my career, success would have come more easily, and I would have been a lot easier to be around. The reason for that is fairly simple to explain – harder to do. The INSEAD course taught me to listen properly, and to time my contributions correctly.

The idea that listening is an art – something, actually, you have to learn – sounds a bit zen, I admit. But it really is a practical skill: you can learn and practise it. It comes down to focus and concentration and control of your own ego. So often, when we're in conversation, we're multitasking, trying to follow what the other person is saying while looking to edge in with our own thoughts. This is a fairly rubbish way to conduct a conversation, and it's positively ruinous in a mentoring environment. That eager multitasker at the back of my brain needs gagging. I need to listen intently, imagining my way into the thoughts of the person who's speaking. My own experiences are useful only to the extent that they are relevant. The deeper I listen, the more empathetic I am, the more I find I have to offer.

One simple, mechanical shortcut to attaining some level of focus and empathy is what we may politely term 'the power of the pause' ('shutting the hell up' may also serve). If, after my client has spoken, I stay silent, for just a few seconds, it generates just enough discomfort that my client will dig deeper, and express themselves just that little bit more. After a while the discomfort goes away, but the pattern remains; the client feels confident in voicing their ideas and worries because they feel, rightly, that I'm paying real attention to them.

I certainly don't think coaching should be forced on people, but it should be made available to anyone who would benefit from it, and we make a point of offering coaching sessions to senior leaders in HomeServe.

When HomeServe was bought by the private equity giant Brookfield Asset Management, we really welcomed having two of their senior people come and work in HomeServe. This helped us understand our owner's culture and how we could get the most help and advice from them. It was also a career opportunity for people in Brookfield who were investors but hadn't been involved in running a business. One of those incomers was Taylor Hall, an experienced finance guy who hadn't run a big team before. We wanted to throw him in at the deep end and give him that responsibility, so we made him CFO at HomeServe EMEA (Europe, Middle East and Africa). To give him extra support, we found him a business coach to help him develop his team management skills. Those sessions really helped him, and convinced me that every manager, at every level, should think about having coaching at some stage in their lives.

NO ONE IS AN ISLAND

Once a year, members of the Procter & Gamble Alumni Network come together to listen to a guest speaker and share experiences as a peer group. We're working in different roles and industries but continue to learn from each other. We're like sleeper cells in a carefully constructed satellite network – you never quite know when a connection will provide valuable insight, but somehow they always do.

As HomeServe grew, I resolved to create a similarly powerful network of talents and ideas. For the past decade, HomeServe's alumni club has served three distinct purposes. First, we learn from each other: once a year, former HomeServe stars return to speak to us about their business experiences – people such as Greg Jackson, who, before he founded Octopus Energy, built our heating installation operation.

Second, the network creates unbreakable connections so people feel there is always a place for them here. We like to say that no one who's great at their job ever leaves HomeServe. We just send them on secondment to get some external learning before they return even more talented – people such as Emma Thomas, now our group general counsel after a period at Britvic.

Third, it leads to business development opportunities. Five years ago, Len Lvovich attended our alumni event. He had left HomeServe to set up Synergym, a low-cost fitness chain in Spain. Talking to him convinced me I needed to know more. I ended up personally investing €6 million in his expansion. Today, he has 107 gyms open and a plan to get to 200 over the next two years.

It staggers me that the King's Trust (formerly the Prince's Trust) has no similar alumni set-up. It's one of the UK's most inspiring organisations for young talent; it has created 125,000 entrepreneurs and provided business support for almost 400,000 more. A formalised network would help so many successful people provide advice, guidance and insight to the next generation of business go-getters.

Networking is most effective when you stop thinking of it as transactional. It should be about what you can give and learn, rather than what you can get and who you can connect with. We're not great at building such networks in the UK, preferring loose arrangements or nudges on LinkedIn. *Business Leader*'s head of membership, Craig Wilmann, was one of the founders of The Leaders Council, a young leaders' organisation, and identifies where the British scene falls short: 'We were interested in networking, but there was no direction, no component to us that specifically helped and encouraged you to grow your business. We had three hundred members at one point, but an open-ended network like that tends to stagnate.'

It's a shame – all you need is a bit of structure, and it's this that I'm trying to provide with my *Business Leader* membership community. *Business Leader* began with a happy accident. The journalist Graham Ruddick had set up his own business newsletter and podcast and was looking to raise money to expand it. He'd already had some offers from venture capital firms when I dropped in to be interviewed for his podcast. I got in touch again a short time later and said I was looking to build something to help medium-sized businesses go from good to great. 'I've bought this little magazine *Business Leader* and I need better content, so why don't we work together? You can expand a lot faster with me than with venture capital money.' Now we have an office in King's Cross with about thirty people, we've got ten editions of the magazine out, a podcast every week and we've laid the foundations to do something special.

As well as a magazine, a newsletter and a podcast, *Business Leader* is a membership community for entrepreneurs and chief executives running businesses that turn over more than £3 million and employ between 15 and 250 staff. (Giant companies should be able to look after themselves, and there are already very many organisations to support start-ups. It's the people in the middle who get repeatedly forgotten.) We're using the peer group model from Vistage and YPO (formerly Young Presidents' Organization), a US-based organisation of chief executives. Both organisations have offshoots in the UK, but neither has managed in a big way to persuade UK CEOs to meet regularly and discuss their challenges. We think we can succeed here where they have not.

Even now I'm still hungry for mentorship. (No matter how successful you are, or think you are, the best way to develop is to listen.) These days I'm learning from the chief executive of a highly successful European private equity house, because I want to learn how to be a better investor. I think more people should have coaches and mentors, but in the UK, the message is still not getting through.

I'm sure that, through *Business Leader,* we can change this. I'm certain that my success with HomeServe would have happened faster and with fewer wrong turns had I been able to turn to such an organisation.

SUMMING UP

Listen your way to growth

Everyone in business needs at least the basics of an entrepreneurial education. Large or small, CEO or independent trader, you've got to keep raising your game: remember, what brought you success in the first place may not get you where you really want to go.

You can't spend your whole time on your own, second-guessing your every decision and worrying about the changes that might be coming around the corner to transform your business. That will just paralyse your ability to make decisions.

You need good counsel. You need the insights of trusted others, and you need the humility to listen to those insights, take them seriously and put them into action.

Seek three kinds of counsel:

Colleagues with expertise offer tactical help in navigating day-to-day challenges and spotting potential problems. Coaches help you understand and tackle your issues and opportunities, and encourage you to hold true to your values as you pursue success. Mentors with broad industry knowledge can take business coaching outputs and add help and advice from their experience.

Be tenacious

Valuable advice is often hard won. Be persistent in seeking mentors and insights, and seize opportunities as they arise. Make that late-night phone call and jump on that flight to Washington! Remember, 'no' usually means 'not yet'.

Mentors don't dictate

Our experiences with Jim Collins showed me that true coaches and mentors don't tell you what to do. They guide you towards discovering your own answers by asking insightful questions and highlighting broader perspectives. They show rather than tell.

Read, read, read . . .

Proven business frameworks (and *How to Make a Billion* is one of them) can offer a structure for growth and transformation when internal insight is limited. An insightful book can be an invaluable mentor, especially when your book of contacts is slim.

Chapter Four

Bricks and Clicks and Paper

HomeServe was born in 1993 into a world where most people didn't even have a mobile phone, let alone a smartphone. What would HomeServe look like if it had to start again from nothing in a digital market? How would a small, nimble start-up get a foothold in the home emergency repairs sector? What tricks were we missing? Who was snapping at our heels?

These were the questions swirling round our heads in the mid-2010s, as we set about developing digital services for our customers: online applications, account management, policy renewals and claims, et cetera. The process did not come as naturally to us as to companies that were, by virtue of their youth, 'digital natives'. I think we felt rather self-conscious, and that led us to make an understandable, but still rather costly, mistake.

We set up a Global Digital Technology Group, and asked it to answer all our difficult questions about how to survive and thrive in a rapidly digitising market. We brought in excellent people, the best in the business, and the work they generated was considerable. Yet the group didn't work. Because it had no direct access to the market, the group had no easy way to test its concepts. We had chosen good people, but we had sealed them up in an ivory tower, where they could only drop untested initiatives onto the heads of people who, without any sense of control or personal investment, had to implement them. We didn't need a group of digital experts sitting together in an office. We needed digital experts everywhere. Part of our digital maturation was, ironically, to abandon and disperse the Digital Technology Group. What we learned then holds even truer today: digital success is about *balancing* our digital offering with our real-world offering.

We need a strategy that combines the real and the virtual. We're not setting up our sales channels in competition with each other; we want them to bring out the best in each other. So, from playing catch-up and feeling like a bit of a dinosaur, HomeServe pivoted to a much more positive customer-focused outlook. The moment a potential customer encountered us, we wanted to give them a seamless 'omnichannel' journey, assembled from 24/7 customer service, personalised communication and the promise of human interaction where needed. That's the kind of strategy that will break down boundaries and truly put the customer at the heart of what you do.

Of course, there are as many flavours of 'omnichannel' success as there are companies brave enough to attempt it. We'll begin this chapter by looking at a few.

THE REAL WORLD, AND HOW TO USE IT

Warby Parker is a bespoke optician in the US that began life as a thriving online-only company. You can choose five frames from the company's website and try them on at home for free, so you can see how they look on you before committing to a purchase. They wear their social conscience on their sleeve, donating spectacles to people in need through their 'Buy a Pair, Give a Pair' programme. Their customer service is considered second to none. And they still manage to undercut their competition.

How do they do this? You might assume it's because they've remained an online-only company, spending on the customer all the money they save on ground rent. The four friends who started the company (after one of them lost his glasses) thought exactly the same way. For three years, Neil Blumenthal, Andrew Hunt, David Gilboa and Jeffrey Raider put off opening a bricks-and-mortar store, afraid it would cannibalise existing online sales in New York.

It did the opposite.

Almost the moment Warby Parker opened its signature store in SoHo, Manhattan, the company's online conversion rate doubled. The number of web visitors in the New York zip codes around the store also went up significantly. The company's credibility increased with a physical presence. Its market cap has since grown to $1.6 billion.

Now, there's more to this story. If Warby Parker had just opened any old spectacles store, I'm sure it wouldn't have met with anything like the same success. But the store in SoHo was anything but run of the mill. It was designed to feel like a library, with bookshelves, ladders and a reference desk-style checkout counter. This is one of those innovations that seem so obvious after the fact that you can't help but wonder why no one thought of it before. What's a leading cause of myopia? Reading. (Sad, but true.) Almost every Warby Parker customer opens a book once in a while, and so the SoHo store spoke immediately to their interests and self-identity. It also marked out Warby Parker from their competition, who were all dressed as clinically as possible, I suppose in an effort to resemble hospital optometrists.

Something I've noticed about the best online companies is that, as they've expanded into bricks and mortar, they've brought a wonderful sense of free expression and inventiveness to the high street. These businesses grew up laser-focused on good design – on visual impact and elegance and seamless user experience – and the best of them have carried these lessons into the material world.

In 2023, Warby Parker stripped out the shelving and ladders from its SoHo store and replaced them with an art gallery showcasing local artists. It's a subtle and effective change of emphasis. Now that Warby Parker has numerous stores across the US and Canada, it doesn't need to announce its affinity with spectacle wearers quite so obviously: it can now adapt its store designs to fit different locations and demographics. And what could be better, in SoHo, given its cultural history, than a gallery showcasing local art?

PARTNERS IN PROFIT

Establishing a physical presence for your online brand doesn't have to mean owning your own storefront. Strategic retail partnerships offer valuable brand-building opportunities, especially these days, given the rising cost of online advertising. Successful stores act as powerful marketing tools in themselves, and if you can establish a strong retail presence in one of them, you might very well find that you don't need to shell out on that eye-wateringly expensive online marketing campaign.

Passenger Clothing is a UK-based outdoor clothing brand that's visibly and measurably committed to sustainability and ethical business practices. It uses responsibly sourced materials like recycled cotton, recycled polyester, hemp and organic cotton in over 90 per cent of its products. For every order placed, it plants a tree.

In the grand 1960s tradition of brands like Patagonia and North Face, Passenger grew out of its founders' enthusiasm for the great outdoors. Richard and Alexa Sutcliffe started Passenger in 2012, after a life-changing trip to the wilderness of British Columbia. The mission statement they came up with is one of the best I've ever encountered. 'Inspire Meaningful Escapism' embraces the sheer fun and pleasure of leaving the beaten track, and at the same time it invites you to think more deeply about what you're doing and why, and what the effects might be. That 'meaningful' is a stroke of genius – it's positively inviting you to plant a few flowers while you're picking them. (I'm talking metaphorically. Don't pick the flowers.)

Passenger is primarily an online retail company. Their website allows them to connect directly with their customers and control their brand message. As I write this, the team are looking at using AI to predict which of their products their customers will purchase next. You won't find a company much more digital-savvy than Passenger.

In 2023, I made my largest ever investment at the time and acquired a 30 per cent shareholding to help fuel the company's further growth and international expansion. (A quarter of its sales now come from overseas.) Steve Hewitt, the former CEO of Gymshark, joined Passenger as non-exec chairman as part of the deal and made an investment himself.

How many bricks-and-mortar Passenger stores have they opened since then? None. How many do they plan on opening in the near future? None. Passenger expands instead through strategic retail partnerships. Its first was with John Lewis, the godfather of ethical retail in the UK. John Lewis stores profit from the Passenger range, and we've found that if people don't find the full range or the right size and go to look for what they want online, they go to Passenger's website rather than John Lewis's. Passenger's strong online presence has in no way been undermined by its association with John Lewis – a company, might I add, with an excellent web store of its own.

Talking to Simon Wolfson, the inspiring chief executive of clothing retail giant Next, gave me an insight into why strategic retail partnerships are so useful for the bricks-and-mortar stores that host them. Next has shown remarkable agility as it adapts to its market's steady migration online. Now it's pivoting to seize the opportunities that are emerging as online expenses skyrocket and ground rents plummet. Retail sales have dropped by nearly 30 per cent in the last ten years, but at the same time rents have come down by enough to allow savvy retailers to keep their shops open. Next had seven hundred shops at its bricks-and-mortar peak. It's still got five hundred. It's managed to maintain that dominant high-street presence in large part through having an omnichannel model.

Next started selling other brands about fifteen years ago. This began with one of their teams saying, 'I think we could sell Nike trainers on our website. Can I try?' (This, incidentally, has always been the mantra at Next: try lots of things in a small way, and if something doesn't work, learn what you can, stop worrying and move on.) Today, strategic retail is a £400 or £500 million business for Next. When Gap lost retail market share in the UK, it closed all its eighty-one stores in the UK and Ireland and migrated to concessions in Next. Retrenchment is never a happy business, but Gap is still a force in UK retail thanks to this partnership.

Next has the same arrangement with Victoria's Secret and Bath & Body Works. It's the franchisee; it runs the retail operations and sells the franchise product, while the franchisor reaps the profit of selling products in the UK.

More recently, Next has pivoted once again, selling other people's brands online via its own website, the 'Total Platform'. Behind this second pivot was Simon Wolfson's realisation that, as the world shifted into online shopping, smaller brands such as Reiss, JoJo Maman Bébé and Laura Ashley might lack the financial power to make the transition easily. Wolfson figured that he could use Next's infrastructure to help them, and boost Next's profits along the way. They have also acquired some brands. (Here's what the merchants of 'cut-throat' business stories never tell you: the best deals you will ever strike are win-win.)

AUTHENTICITY WINS . . .

If you're a pure bricks-and-mortar business, your customer base will be decided largely by geography. A hyper-specialised shop might draw footfall from all over the world. An acquaintance of mine lives next door to a man who hand-fashions snooker cues. He's only made the local press once – the day the Sultan of Brunei popped round with a broken cue.

Needless to say, these kinds of businesses are extreme outliers. Most of the time, you're drawing footfall from an area no larger than is comfortably covered by your local bus network. Not so for companies that have achieved omnichannel success. For omnichannel businesses, online affiliations can draw customers to a bricks-and-mortar store from much further afield to attend an event, a celebrity appearance, a learning opportunity, or even a workout session. The challenge for these businesses is to offer a great in-store experience that adds to an already winning online journey and online store.

Ben Francis co-founded Gymshark in 2012 with his friend Lewis Morgan when he was just nineteen. They started the business from his parents' garage while he was still a student and delivering pizzas. Gymshark grew rapidly, thanks primarily to its use of social media marketing and its partnerships with fitness influencers.

'We're a community-led brand,' Ben explains, 'and it's a community based around an activity rather than a location. We need to make sure that every store attracts a community that's large enough and engaged enough to sustain it. We have to test; we can't afford to make too many sweeping assumptions. As a consequence, I'd rather have too few stores than too many.

'Another reason we move slowly and steadily is my ambition for Gymshark to be a hundred-year brand. I grew up in Birmingham, hearing stories about companies like Cadbury and Land Rover. They inspired me to try and make Gymshark stand the test of time. Whenever we take at risk, we think, "What would a hundred-year brand do?" I don't think they'd run as quickly as they can at something for five years with the risk that it could all go wrong. They'd be more considered. Slowness is not that much of a disadvantage, if you're sure you're moving in the right direction.'

Gymshark actually began life as an IRL ('in real life', i.e., non-digital) brand, serving a small community of enthusiasts. 'For a community brand like ours,' Ben says, 'the flow between channels is never one-way. Our main job at the moment is to entice people who met us online to visit us in real life, and because of that, people think we're an online brand that's making a go of bricks and mortar. In fact, our business originated offline, by us organising events in Ohio, LA, Melbourne, Birmingham and Cologne – all before we got a name for ourselves on the internet. It was people who attended our weight-lifting sessions who first followed us online, and helped build our online following. Opening stores is more a return to our roots, but at a much bigger scale.'

Now that Gymshark is expanding in to bricks and mortar, I wondered if its relationship with its influencers had changed? Gymshark is famous for making excellent use of social media endorsements. Generally, though, influencer marketing isn't nearly as good as it used to be. It's the same with any channel: when it's new, it's disproportionately valuable, but as it becomes more popular, it settles to a more realistic value.

Ben isn't fazed: 'It's easy to confuse the medium and the message. Influencer marketing isn't new. When members of the royal family came to visit to Birmingham, everyone in the Jewellery Quarter would throw their goods at them – literally *throw them* – hoping something of theirs would catch the royal eye. Social media has certainly expanded influencer culture, and it's still massively valuable for us and for others, but like everything else, it's constantly evolving.

'Influencer marketing is a no-brainer for us because we're in the inspiration and encouragement business. The gym industry is all about helping clients improve physically and mentally, and we are firmly rooted in that culture. So, we work with the best bodybuilders in the world. Two of the three winners at Mr. Olympia a few weeks ago were Gymshark athletes. They're our core influencers, and with them at our centre, we also work with people who go to the gym five days a week, not because they'll ever be world champions, but because they are dedicated to the gym and what it can do for their mental and physical health. Wherever you are on your fitness journey, there's someone speaking for our brand, pushing you to the next level.'

These days, 'influencer culture' has become almost synonymous with superficiality and insincerity. Throw a stick into social media, and you will hit a business handling influencers in ways ranging from the counterproductive to the positively embarrassing. Victoria Lynch of Additional Lengths finds influencers are very useful to her business, but she despairs of the use they're generally put to in her industry. 'Some companies rely on gimmicks and hype to create short-term buzz. I believe in staying true to my word and building trust over time. We've achieved success through strong values, product quality and genuine customer relationships. I don't want to manipulate customers. I want them to trust our brand because of the quality and value we provide. Why invest in something that's just a fleeting trend?

'And that, in a nutshell, is why I've never relied on influencer culture. If social media disappeared tomorrow, I want us still to be standing strong. Sure, the temptation is there: one of our competitors has built their entire business that way. But I think it's a short-sighted approach. Our competitor saw their revenues decline last year, and we're pretty sure it's because they relied too heavily on influencer marketing, even as that approach is becoming less effective.

'Social media is important, and we use it to reach our target audience, but full-on influencer marketing on its own is not a sustainable strategy. If people buy things based on hype and endorsements, they can't help but be disappointed with the actual product. No wonder consumers are becoming more sceptical.

'Even though we don't sell large volumes directly to consumers, we're number one with trade professionals. They're a loyal customer base that depends on us, and there's no more solid foundation. Because we began our business selling to professionals, it's second nature to us to focus on quality products and genuine customer relationships. And if now we have an opportunity to explore influencer marketing, we'll do it strategically, and on our own terms.

'Influencers help us reach new customers, but we'll do it by collaborating with people who have real cachet in the industry. Our biggest influencers are the trade professionals who use and recommend our products. They're not paid to promote us; they genuinely believe in our brand. That's a wonderful endorsement. We don't need to pay celebrities millions of dollars.'

True strength lies in value, not hype. Hype is about jacking up the weekly numbers. Value is about establishing relationships with people. Now I don't mean to get too starry-eyed about this. In business we handle numbers all the time. Working at the scale we do, we haven't got much choice in the matter. But if you can only hang on to the idea that, behind those numbers, your market consists of people, you'll save yourself from many errors.

Above all, you will understand that authenticity builds lasting trust; manufactured trends are bound, sooner or later, to crumble.

. . . AND SO DOES SIMPLICITY

Having established the case for omnichannel businesses, I should now come clean and tip my hat to a glaring counter-example: a business that hasn't embraced an omnichannel strategy, and still does spectacularly well for itself. I think this business is an outlier, but I can't and shouldn't ignore it. It is, if you like, the exception that proves the rule.

Simon Arora, the CEO of discount retail store B&M, has no time for online. Their shops are so well bedded in their communities that B&M doesn't even use TV advertising. At the age of twenty-five, Simon and his younger brother Bobby set up Orient Sourcing Services. The idea was to import housewares and home furnishings from Asia and supply everyone in the UK, from superstores such as Tesco and B&Q through to independent shopkeepers. They imported just about everything – kitchenware, tableware, housewares, bed linen, towels, rugs and throws – and by the time they sold up they had reached the bottom rungs of the *Sunday Times* Rich List.

'Finding the next venture was simply a matter of searching through the records of Companies House for a retail business of a certain size,' Simon recalls. 'I didn't want to do another start-up. I needed something with a minimum turnover of five to ten million.' What he found was a chain of twenty-one somewhat scruffy bargain shops dotted around the north-west of England. 'It was losing a couple of million pounds a year, and would run out of cash within six to eight weeks, which is how I picked it up for around half a million.'

There's another reason B&M was going so cheap. It was the autumn of 2004, slap-bang in the middle of the global recession, and national retail chains were starting to go bust, one after the other, including stores such as Kwiksave, Comet and JJB. Everyone in the industry knew that at some point Woolworths, the granddaddy of them all, was likely to fail. A third of its sales were in CDs, videos and DVDs, and all these products were migrating online. In December 2008 Woolworths collapsed into administration, and its stores came up for grabs. It's a perfect example of how a dislocation – and the 2008 financial crisis was certainly that – creates opportunities for an upstart.

Simon and Bobby bought Woolworths, brought in new people to help them broaden their offer and invested in IT to make their already super-simple supply chain even more efficient. By 2023, B&M's profit had risen from £3 million to £600 million. 'We evolved a bricks-and-mortar model that doesn't need click and collect, or, indeed, much online presence at all,' says Simon with evident pride. 'We kept our model as simple as possible so we could remain as agile and disruptive as possible. We concentrated all our efforts on pricing and range selection. We're on-trend, our stock availability is second to none and we can win on price.'

So here's the acid test for the omnichannel model I was talking about: B&M was built over seventeen to eighteen years of consecutive revenue growth, and they achieved this entirely through word of mouth. 'That's the most cost-effective marketing, and the cheapest,' says Simon Arora. 'As a business family we had absolutely no experience of, or competence in, advertising, and early on we decided to direct the 2 per cent we ought to have spent on advertising into something we were good at: pricing.'

Once you do that, and find yourself looking at advertising from the outside, the figures do become eye-watering: 'B&M looks for a 10 per cent profit margin. So, from our point of view, for every million pounds you spend on advertising, you will need to generate £10 million of turnover to break even.' How many adverts achieve that?

B&M doesn't have a complex calendar of promotions where suddenly things are being sold two-for-one or three-for-two. It doesn't do points or loyalty schemes. B&M offers us the same every-day low price wherever we are and whether we're coming in once or a hundred times. 'We've shied away from selling clothing because we don't want changing rooms,' says Simon. 'We've steered clear of frozen food so we don't have freezers and chiller cabinets cluttering up the store.' It's true enough: dedicated customer service desks and in-store cafes and shop window displays are nice to have, but they all add complexity, processes and, ultimately, cost. B&M doesn't need them.

'Every management consultant, every observer, every analyst will say: you have to be omnichannel, multichannel and click and collect. You don't have to be any of these things,' Simon insists, 'and in any event, you absolutely shouldn't underestimate the complexity and cost they'll bring to your every transaction. Argos is a wonderful store, the undisputed king of click and collect. You can buy things from a catalogue, wherever you happen to be. You can go to a store to collect them, or even have them delivered. It's a big business – a really big business; it turns over probably £4 billion a year – but I honestly can't remember the last time its profits earned a headline.

'Every time you buy a £5 toy from one of our stores, we earn £1.50. That £1.50 goes towards the rent, our colleagues' wages and all the business of getting the toy into the right shop at the right time. If, alongside that, I want to offer you the ability to go online, pick out what you want and collect it from the store at three o'clock tomorrow, what has to happen? Well, at the bare minimum, a warehouse operative has to go to a shelf in the depot, pick out that one toy, get it onto a roll cage and make sure it's overnighted to the store. Then it's got to be taken off the lorry, put somewhere, and then when the customer arrives, someone's got to find it for them and give it to them. All for £1.50? You just can't do it. The only way you can earn £1.50 is if the customer spots it on a shelf, picks it out, goes to the till and pays: job done.'

By embracing a business model of extreme simplicity, and by sticking rigidly to that model, B&M leaves the shopper with the distinct impression that it's not being greedy. That's B&M's USP in a nutshell: it's a store that serves its community. Its stores are found quite often in relatively deprived neighbourhoods, providing employment where jobs are often in short supply, and offering goods that people on low incomes can afford. B&M grew so fast that over a period of six years it created more jobs than any other private company in the UK. Today it employs over 42,000 colleagues, many in otherwise struggling high streets in working-class neighbourhoods.

Now: what could an omnichannel strategy add to that? As of today? Nothing. B&M offers a powerful riposte to the omnichannel argument, I think you'll agree. So let me now reply to it . . .

COMBINING STRENGTHS

Limited assortment discounters have only limited use for online as it's currently conceived. Part of this is to do with how limited assortment discounters work. But I think it's also to do with how online advertising works at the moment. The cost of online advertising, particularly through platforms like Google, is already very high and is likely to go on increasing.

When you go to Google now, you need to scroll quite a way to find a site that isn't sponsored. Pinpointing customers who are likely to respond to adverts is now a business priority. The fashion giant Next has invested quite aggressively in understanding the technology behind social media and Google advertising, and as I write this, it's just doubled its marketing expenditure. It's had to: a bigger percentage of its transactions are now driven by online advertising, as natural search diminishes.

'Online advertising costs a fortune now,' HomeServe's former managing director Jonathan King complains. 'Google has found a way to extract all the profit out of any market. As soon as a market becomes profitable, they increase the cost of the relevant search words. I was chairman of an energy company in Manchester, and I remember us testing some new pages. "Don't whatever you do click that blue button," the managing director begged me. He explained it cost us £50 every time someone clicked on the ad, because Google's algorithm was on the case and increased the company's fee with every click-through.'

The online marketplace has become incredibly price-competitive, an all-against-all race to the bottom, making it difficult to stand out and maintain profit margins. To be brutally honest, I think B&M is right to stay out of this game.

However, I very much doubt that this environment is sustainable. In the long run, the market will have to self-correct. In a healthier digital environment, I think even B&M, which focuses entirely on physical stores and their offerings on-site, might eventually benefit from an online strategy driving home deliveries, and not just a website and an online presence that drives customers to their stores.

The key to a successful omnichannel strategy lies in understanding the key strengths of each channel. These will change over time, so it's important to keep researching and adapting.

Right now, bricks and mortar are a lasting, cost-effective investment, their physical presence a constant form of advertising, creating familiarity and trust. Clicks are very expensive in comparison, and you don't ever want to be spending your business's hard-earned money on mere 'nice-to-haves'. That, however, is no reason to abandon online channels. Rather, you want to look for what the online channel can do that IRL channels cannot. You want to hunt down, and focus on, the specific strengths of each channel.

Online can be so much more than a bottomless money pit for your advertising spend. After years of 'digital revolution', it's at last beginning to dawn on us all that the internet at its best (and at its most profitable) *extends and enriches* the real world, rather than attempting to replace it. Here's an example of what I mean, drawn from my work at Growth Partner.

In December 2020 we acquired a significant minority stake in Cubico Group, the parent company of Easy Bathrooms. This was Craig Waddington's second bathrooms company; the first, founded by his twin brother, who had since died, was wrested away from Craig by a predatory bank. (This is a whole other can of worms, and one I'll be sure to revisit.) 'When we set up Cubico,' Craig recalls, 'I thought we'd begin by doing some online retailing. That's the easiest business to get going, right? I understood the bathroom market better than anybody in the industry, so I figured I'd be able to sell all around the country from my website.

'Our first hurdle was finding a name. Every single name was gone. You'd think of a name as an online retailer, and it was already taken. Lots of companies buy names and then sell them on like number plates. We finally stumbled on 'Easy Bathrooms' and couldn't quite believe it was still available. It still cost us $2,000, mind. Meanwhile, we had opened a second shop, paid for by selling my car for a BMX. I'd cycle to work in the second shop while my wife operated the first.'

As for the online business – well, there was good news and bad news. The good news was that, knowing the business as well as he did, Craig could outcompete his online competition on price. The bad news was that he couldn't even begin to compete on marketing spend.

'I couldn't quite believe what I was seeing; there were these huge companies doing a hundred million turnover, and they would be spending ten million a year with Google!

'We opened a third shop and called it Easy Bathrooms. By the third month it was profitable. A fourth shop followed. Again, we called it Easy Bathrooms. And again, by the third month it was turning a profit. And that's when it dawned. I didn't have to compete on marketing spend. I could outcompete my online rivals *using showrooms.*'

Craig's view of online business culture is cutting in the extreme. 'People talk about internet commerce as if it's full of energy and innovation. I think a lot of internet-only people have no fire in their belly at all. Back in 2004, if you didn't want to do what my brother and I did – open a retail shop and travel the country and work seven days a week – then you called yourself an online retailer. You could close your laptop on a Friday and reopen it on a Monday and miraculously the technology would pick up the slack. Twenty years later and while you're paying through the nose for every advert, I'm out there in the cold and the wet, stealing your business.

'The internet is never going to go away, but I think we have more opportunities to help Easy Bathrooms online because we've got the stores. It used to be, you could go into our stores, feel and touch the products, and then buy them on someone else's website. These days you visit our website, design your bathroom and come visit our stores to see it come alive in front of you. "Here, touch this tile! Try this tap!"'

In 2022, and alongside Lloyds Banking Group, we gave Easy Bathrooms further funding to support their continued expansion. As part of that process the company has a new CEO, Adrian Burleton. Adrian, who has a background in retail, online and home shopping, is even now overseeing a fresh omnichannel strategy that combines a great network of stores, convenient online purchasing and a super-reliable delivery system.

Easy Bathrooms have found that merely selling bathroom suites online is difficult. 'The online market is so price driven,' Craig explains. 'Customers online compare prices from multiple retailers and generally plump for the cheapest option; they imagine this saves them time and fuss, as well as money.'

For myself, I'd want to take more time over such a serious, one-off expense. And this is why I think Easy Bathrooms's website is such a winner. It's less a sales portal, more a way to inspire customers and get them started on their bathroom renovation plans. They can browse the company's products, get ideas and submit measurements of their space. Then, when they visit the showroom, Easy Bathrooms's expert staff can provide personalised design advice and help them create what they're after within their budget.

Wren Kitchens, another home improvement business I really admire, has adopted a similar model: their online presence is there to inform and inspire, while the physical showrooms provide one-to-one design and sales consultations. The approach – which we can now see being copied across the home improvements sector – plays to the strengths of both online and physical retail. The internet is too intangible a medium to ever work brilliantly as a complete sales platform for major purchases like a kitchen or bathroom. It is, however, a superb and unrivalled search tool. So why not play to digital strengths, and create a site that the consumer can usefully and enjoyably explore? Customers will then complete their journey at a physical store, where authentic, personalised service and salesmanship come into their own.

ALL BUSINESS IS SHOW BUSINESS

HomeServe has to work very hard to connect tangibly with its customers. It is, after all, an insurance business. Until the boiler breaks or a pipe bursts, the peace of mind offered by HomeServe membership is intangible – no more than a piece of paper, or perhaps an email. That's why HomeServe puts such emphasis on the excellence of its call centres, engineers and follow-up processes. This might be the company's only chance to deliver on all its promises, and even then it can only ever be as good as its worst engineer on their worst day.

What HomeServe lacks, or has lacked until recently, is 'bricks'. There's no place you can go to see what HomeServe does, or witness its workmanship, or examine the tools of its trade – its boilers, its air-conditioning units, its solar panels. But this may be about to change, given HomeServe's new post-sale focus on decarbonising your home.

I promise I'll come back to the sheer cost of decarbonising your home later on. The other thing homeowners need is the chance to see what this all-new technology, that everybody in a suit wants them to have installed in their home, looks like.

Not an unreasonable request, is it? And yet, in the UK, all this extraordinary technology is sitting around in labs and warehouses, not even being demonstrated, not even being *shown* to the people who are being expected to buy it. The UK government has set a target of 600,000 heat-pump installations a year by 2028. In 2024, only 60,000 were installed. It's not that the public are suspicious of the new technology. It's worse than that: they are not being given a clue what the new technology *is*. Homeowners rightly want to see this stuff first-hand before committing. So why don't we have heating shops? They do in Spain. Endesa, a major Spanish energy company, operates installer-run service points, and these places are getting a surprisingly high footfall. HomeServe's Spanish operation, which includes acquired heating installation businesses, has been quick to adopt this model. Its shops showcase boilers, heat pumps and, increasingly, battery storage and solar solutions.

Could we replicate this success in the UK with stores proudly sporting the HomeServe name and using the expertise of BOXT, our online boiler and renewable energy installation business, now that it's part of HomeServe? Imagine a dedicated space where customers can experience these technologies first-hand!

CUT THROUGH THE NOISE

Wine from Laithwaites. Bedding from The White Company. Shirts from Charles Tyrwhitt. Exercise gear from Sweaty Betty (not for me, that one). I'm a sucker for a well-produced mailshot and catalogue.

Fewer businesses are using direct mail these days, which means those that do get more attention on the doormat, especially from those people who are still working from home a few days a week.

And it doesn't stop with the materials addressed directly to me. It dawned on me the other day, as I looked in on our local high street, that the stores I entered were the ones that had leafleted me. It wasn't so long ago that mailshots were the bane of our lives. 'No junk mail!' signs were everywhere – and no wonder, given how much of the stuff was poorly targeted and badly written. And all the while – remember this? – we'd be poring over our PCs, waiting with bated breath for that vital personal email. Well, the more things change, the more they stay the same. Our email inboxes are now so full of junk, many mail servers sort it into different types before it even reaches us. Online ad blocking is becoming more sophisticated. Digital advertising costs are soaring.

But that unsolicited material slipped into our physical postboxes? It's actually getting better. Pause by the bin next time and open this stuff up and take a look. You don't have to buy anything. (A successful direct mail campaign rarely garners more than one in one hundred responses.) But I want you to see, with your own eyes, what is happening. The real world is making a comeback.

Don't just take my word for it. Johnnie Boden called himself a 'nitwit' for ditching the Boden catalogue, a mistake that helped turn a £22 million profit in 2022 into a £4.4 million loss a year later. Resurrecting his company's paper catalogue, he believes, was one of the best decisions he's made since launching the fashion brand in 1991.

As a marketeer, there's a lot to love about direct mail. And don't just take my word for it. Here's Jonathan King again: 'I love the direct part of direct mail. With direct mail, you can measure, with absolute certainty, what's working and what's not. [He's right. Remember that I first realised HomeServe's membership model would be successful after I received thirty-eight responses from sending out a thousand mailshots. If that hadn't happened, the business would have stalled before it had even got started.] And once your campaign is working,' he goes on, 'you can know exactly how much you're spending and how much it will bring back.'

It's not all about the paper, of course. As Jonathan points out, other direct-response campaigns are available: 'In the US, we do some TV advertising now, but it's a direct-response campaign, with Tom Rusin, our CEO, in the role of Honest Joe, telling you to "Call that number now!" It's great fun and, to my surprise [Jonathan is currently chairman of HomeServe's Japanese operation], the Japanese respond really well to that approach. Never mind brand building, let's get people on the phones, learning about us direct!'

Mind you, sometimes paper really *is* the magic ingredient. 'Print has a huge USP [unique selling point],' says Graham Ruddick, editor-in-chief of *Business Leader*. 'It gives our work a premium feel and status. For our audience, who are constantly travelling, having the magazine on sale in WHSmith in airports and train stations has huge appeal.' From a marketing perspective, paper is a shoo-in: 'It's difficult to get your product in front of someone digitally unless they go looking for it; you can just give someone a magazine.'

So it never ceases to amaze me when dynamic young entrepreneurs look at me in puzzlement as I ask the question: 'How are you targeting customers with printed direct marketing?' As their mentor or investor, once we've discussed their brilliant idea and I've sat through all their plans involving the latest digital technologies, I like to blindside them with my enthusiasm for old-fashioned Royal Mail. More often than not, by the time we've finished, print has risen nearly to the top (if not the very top) of their to-do list. The clincher comes when I tell them that direct mail still accounts for over half of HomeServe's new memberships each year.

There's this lazy assumption that everyone in this digital-savvy world has a smartphone glued to one hand and a tablet glued to the other. The online world may be all around us, but that does not mean your customers are immersed in it. Their analogue world may be an equally effective way to amplify your message, drive engagement and achieve growth. So instead of looking up at the screen, look down at the doormat.

According to a study published by the UK Data & Marketing Association (DMA), 70 per cent of consumers feel that direct mail is more personal than online interactions, with a response rate that's forty times higher.* Neuroscientists have found that direct mail is easier to process mentally than email, engagement is longer, and there is an astonishing 70 per cent increase in brand recall. When your client receives their purchases, there should always be a catalogue in the box prompting their next buy, or (taking a leaf out of Passenger's book) a single personalised leaflet that has used AI to predict what next item the customer is likely to choose. It's also easy to measure how much impact your mailshots are having by encouraging purchases through a brochure's voucher code.

If you have bricks-and-mortar stores, mailshots extend and enrich the in-store experience. That's especially true in the home improvements industry. Catalogues showing the whole product range are a vital part of the in-store sales process for Wren Kitchens and Easy Bathrooms.

Personally, I would steer clear of outbound telemarketing and door-to-door sales. They can all too often feel awkward and intrusive. Telemarketing does have value when you're offering 'sales through service', though – that is, suggesting an extra product or service to a customer who has called your business anyway. They may well be open to hearing about an offer, once their initial query has been well handled.

HomeServe drives sales through service in partnership with utility call centres. When a customer contacts their utility provider about a billing enquiry or to notify them of a move, the call centre agent asks if they have HomeServe coverage. If not, they can transfer the customer to our call centre, where we can explain our services and offer the customer a plan.

We've also seen growth in online acquisitions, but here, interestingly, customers do exactly on our site what we see them do

---

* 1 DMA (2018) 'Direct mail: the bottom line', 20 July. Available online at https://dma.org.uk/article/direct-mail-the-bottom-line. The study used statistics from www.marketreach.co.uk.

elsewhere on the internet: they use the site to search for the cheapest product. Only later, once they've grown familiar with our service, do they upgrade to a more comprehensive plan. Oh well, we can always hurry them along with a mailshot.

A BALANCING ACT

One of the oddest-looking omnichannel businesses I ever came across is one I am now invested in. I'll give you the full story here because it's a great example of how a business evolves to balance online and real-world operations, and how even a company that manifests entirely as paper directories and web pages finds a use, in the end, for bricks and mortar.

The company's called Checkatrade, and, if you're in the UK, I am sure you know our jingle. But we don't start the story there. We start with a phone call in 2016, telling me about a US company called HomeAdvisor. 'It's like an online platform for finding a local trade,' a friend explained. I took a look and was immediately interested. I wondered at the time whether there was anyone like that in the UK. I commissioned an online survey and asked people who bought stuff online, 'If you needed someone to put in a new kitchen or bathroom, where online would you go to get the service you need?' I was doing my market research, but I honestly expected everyone to just say they searched on Google. No: the number-one place they went to was Checkatrade.

I looked into the company and liked what I saw, though it was clear enough that the founder, Kevin Byrne, had taken the company just about as far as he could on his own, and the business was crying out for investment. I went to see Kevin and we had a great meeting, right up until the final bombshell: 'I can't tell you much more, other than that I'm selling my business next week to a big American media group.' Well, I thought, I'm not letting that happen. Anyone armed with Checkatrade might one day challenge HomeServe's core business model. (The American would-be purchaser turned out to be HomeAdvisor!)

So I went back to Kevin and waved the flag. 'Sell to a fellow British entrepreneur, not to those horrible Americans!' was not quite what I said, but I came pretty close. Then I had to muster the courage to go to my board and explain why I wanted to spend £74 million on a company that made only about £1 million a year. Incredibly, they had the courage to back me.

Checkatrade is an awakening giant of digital marketplaces. Last year it broke through the £100 million revenue barrier and cleared £20 million of profit. (That's EBITDA profit, incidentally – what we gained before interest, taxes, depreciation and amortisation. EBITDA's a fairly standard business metric, which, like any metric, can be used to bamboozle people – let's not have any of that here!) More exciting, from my point of view, we've got a five-year plan that we think will grow that figure exponentially. When Brookfield bought HomeServe, I reinvested £20 million of my own money back into Checkatrade to make me a co-owner with Brookfield and chairman of the business.

Checkatrade was born in 1998, the year Kevin Byrne's home town of Selsey in West Sussex suffered a double blow – first a tornado, and then a plague of piratical rogue traders, out to take advantage of the town's misfortune. Kevin's interest in helping out frantic homeowners wasn't just an idea, it was a passion, fuelled by personal experience.

Kevin's response to the rogue trader problem was Scout, a vetted trades directory launched in 1998. When Kevin took that offering online, he renamed it Checkatrade. In 2017, HomeServe acquired the business.

Growing Checkatrade is a delicate business: we are, after all, juggling with the livelihoods of tens of thousands of small businesses and independent tradespeople. We promise them a lot: a brand new online market, fuelled by home improvement and repairs leads from homeowners. But it has to be paid for, and ultimately it has to be paid for out of the pockets of trades who live on a knife's edge of profit and loss.

Checkatrade helps consumers find reliable and vetted trades-people while providing a platform for tradespeople to showcase their work. It distributes nearly 100 million printed directory leaflets a year. Why? Because it's psychologically the right thing to do. When something is tangibly broken or unsatisfactory in their home, some customers would sooner go to our leaflet than surf the internet.

In the public mind, then, Checkatrade has become the internet company that you can still find, a bit creased and battered, stuffed in the back of your kitchen drawer or behind a fridge magnet, in the form of a proper paper directory. A company with digital reach, which still retains a reassuring physical presence.

Underneath Checkatrade's swanlike progress, there's a lot of paddling going on. For everything Checkatrade does to help their trades, the team has to think about what it means for homeowners. Getting the balance right involves collecting information. Checkatrade handles over 4 million jobs every year and gets over 3.5 million visits to its website every month. Most leads going to trades are telephone calls generated by our leaflets and from our online marketplace, and we track every call to see how many each trade is getting, whether they are being answered and how quickly. We now also send our trades quote requests, so they can contact the customer and convert enquiries into completed jobs.

Checkatrade works with seventy-two trade categories, and it doesn't stop there: searches are actually conducted at the subcategory level, and there are over eight hundred of those. Add in local differences and now Checkatrade is trying to match supply and demand across millions of permutations. And all this makes Checkatrade both a powerful digital workhorse and a friendly real-world broker of home improvements and repairs.

Checkatrade used to charge a single annual fee for all trades. This wasn't ideal: whether you were a sole trade or a small business employing six engineers, you were still paying the same membership fee. So, we moved to a monthly pricing model based on your trade and the volume of leads you could handle. We also have a per-lead model for larger trades and national businesses wanting a higher volume of leads. We might even move to a bidding model, where trades can pay more for certain leads, while for smaller jobs we'll set fixed prices and take a modest percentage of the job value.

The trick is to turn a decent profit while providing value for our members. The chief hurdle to that is less about us getting the model wrong – we can always (and we always do) tweak the model. It's more that sole trades and small businesses get very nervous around change. Their liquidity is generally low, so they quite understandably treat every change as a potential threat. I'm not criticising. Small businesses are precarious, so they're right to be wary. But it means that at Checkatrade, we need to be focused on how to build trust and happy customers in a difficult environment.

We're long past the worst; the initial reluctance has receded, and we're offering enough of a range of options and services that our trade partners can choose the model that suits them. We have absolutely no interest in taking our customers over or doing the work ourselves (a possibility that must surely have crossed our clients' minds in the very early days). On the contrary, we partner with trades to help them grow.

The UK economy desperately needs more small businesses and skilled tradespeople, and we can help with that. At the moment, for instance, we're investing heavily in tech people to develop software that will help these businesses run better, integrating quotations, invoicing, payments collection and diary management. This software is for all trades, and if you're a sole trader, it comes bundled with your monthly membership.

As I've already said (maybe more than once), I don't believe in pure online businesses. I reckon a strong online presence needs to be complemented by a physical one, and we're exploring various ways to achieve this with Checkatrade. Could we, for instance, take the concept of the Ideal Home Exhibition – a big UK showcase for the latest domestic designs and inventions – and bring it to local communities? Imagine a home improvement fair in every village and town hall, where homeowners can connect with thirty of our top tradespeople from Checkatrade twice a year. This would allow them to explore options for their next project, while local businesses showcase their services and build relationships.

It's just an idea for now, and the final decision rests with Checkatrade's leadership, but while I'm on the subject, another concept we're exploring is 'Renovation Street' – a retail mall bringing together various home improvement businesses under one roof. This would create a one-stop shop for renovations. After all, remodelling a kitchen might also involve flooring, tiling and even heating upgrades. And if you've done your kitchen this month, you're quite likely to do your bathroom in a year's time. Customers might be inspired to tackle other projects after seeing related businesses in close proximity.

This 'Renovation Street' fosters collaboration and cross-promotion, creating a dynamic hub for home improvement. We're going to see whether we can bring such a thing together and make it happen.

MUST YOU BE COOL?

Whether digital culture has benefited how companies present themselves to the public is a glass-half-full, glass-half-empty sort of question. For every influencer-related catastrophe on social media, there's a Warby Parker or a Gymshark bringing a much-missed sense of place and occasion to the high street.

According to the British Retail Consortium, around 14 per cent of stores sit unloved on our tacky and depressing high streets.[*] Yet there are pockets of positivity. Poole in Dorset is enticing independent retailers back, as is Hebden Bridge's small shops movement in my home county of Yorkshire. Recently, Oxford Street – the nation's most famous shopping street – got in on the act, as Westminster City Council promised entrepreneurs a six-month, rent-free chance to build their brands there and conjure up some desperately needed regeneration.

What's striking is how digital-savvy these operations are. Their interiors are full of reclaimed and repurposed materials and laptops,

[*] Cited in Grimwood, G. *et al.* (2021) 'Town centre regeneration', House of Commons Library, 13 December. Available online at https://researchbriefings.files.parliament.uk/documents/CBP-9218/CBP-9218.pdf.

wherever you look. They're using technology to gather data, to measure customer numbers and footfall frequency per hour, per day, per week. They know how long you stayed, and they know how much you bought. They're using online to extend your customer journey, long after the pop-up has disappeared. They're using it to bring virtual communities to real-life events. They're using it to gather your feedback, and they're using it to stay nimble enough to respond to it. They're using it to monitor their online sales in the catchment area before, during and after their six-month residency. Chances are they'll find they didn't, after all, cannibalise their online experience. Most likely, their online business grew and conversion increased because they linked digital with bricks and mortar.

Online, at its best, extends and enriches the real world. It doesn't replace the real world, and it certainly doesn't need to improve on it. One of the great disservices digital culture has done is to convince businesses large and small that glamour is everything – an essential marketing tool. Does your business really need to be 'cool'? What about your offering is uniquely valuable? Make that element visible and, so far as I'm concerned, bravo – your job is done. (The new generation of pop-up entrepreneurs are brilliant at this.)

'Marketing teams are often tempted to go for what you might call "lifestyle advertising",' says Jonathan King, 'something that shows a happy family with their problems all solved. We've tried that in other markets and it just doesn't work as well as what we actually use to advertise our services – whether it's a jet of water coming out of your lawn from a burst pipe, or water coming through the ceiling and a frazzled homeowner collecting it in a bucket.'

Not every business needs to look as if it just invented the smartphone. On the contrary, it's been my experience that, as tools of persuasion, honesty and directness are far more powerful.

SUMMING UP

It's a question of balance

Real-world interactions create lasting customer connections. While digital tools offer undeniable benefits, they often lack the personal touch that physical experiences provide. Tangible engagements, such as in-person consultations, well-designed retail spaces and even printed materials, foster a deeper level of engagement and brand recall. Strike a balance between digital strategies and real-world initiatives, and you will craft a truly customer-centric business.

Don't neglect traditional marketing

As the Checkatrade story demonstrates, direct mail and physical media still hold value, especially these days, when online channels are oversaturated. These forms of advertising stand out and can foster stronger brand recognition.

Omnichannel strategy is key

Businesses need a cohesive blend of online and offline presence. A well-designed strategy lets each channel reinforce the other, giving the customer the best experience possible. And don't assume you know already what that experience is! Collect and analyse data from both your online and offline interactions to understand your customers better.

Problem-solving is more powerful than glamour

Don't rely on lifestyle-based advertising. Focus your marketing on the problems you can solve for your customers. For example, you may think haircare must be a rather trivial business – but you'd be wildly wrong. Additional Lengths's success is based entirely on taking its customers' needs seriously.

Chapter Five

Hire Your Replacement

Many entrepreneurs have extraordinary difficulty separating themselves from their work. Obsessed by the idea of leaving a personal legacy, they labour their way into the ground and expect others to follow their example. CEOs are just as bad. According to the management consultancy McKinsey, about half of chief executives fail to add value to their organisations because they're too self-obsessed to get the best out of their teams.*

Our businesses are not just our personal legacy. They matter, deeply, to others. And if we're leaders at all, we have to see that we're not here just to advance ourselves. Our job is to inspire people to follow us, to take on our responsibilities and, ultimately, to take our places.

I hire people in the expectation and hope that they're smarter than I am. I want to learn from them, and I want to be able to delegate to them so I can stop working *in* my businesses and start working *on* them. It's easy to get tunnel vision and become controlling when you're building a business. I've been there myself. But learning to let go and trust the people you hire is crucial. Success is a shared journey, and it's important to acknowledge everyone's contributions. The company you build is its own entity, not just an extension of yourself.

My early hires weren't always the wisest, and I procrastinated horribly over one of the best decisions I ever made – hiring Barry

---

* McKinsey & Company (2024) 'Better together: three ways to boost board–CEO collaboration', 25 September. Available online at www.mckinsey.com/capabilities/strategy-and-corporate-finance/our-insights/better-together-three-ways-to-boost-board-ceo-collaboration.

Gibson as a non-exec director in 2004. Over his time with us, the market capitalisation of HomeServe rose from £300 million to over £4 billion, but for a lot of that time, he insists on reminding me, he was just a run-of-the-mill non-executive director. 'Not only that, but I really had to fight for my position. You turned me down for that job three times!' I remember this. I thought Barry was just too corporate and straight-laced. I was after a sir or a lord, someone with a ludicrous pedigree who would impress in meetings. You can imagine the unmitigated disaster that could have been: some of those kinds of people come with an ego.

These days, in making my hires and selecting my appointments, I follow two golden rules. First, I take past performance very seriously. Second- or third-time bosses are often the best – people such as Octopus Energy's Greg Jackson, who is on his third chief executive role and has been highly successful.

Second, try to do as much as you can using the Procter & Gamble approach to hiring: promote people from within. That's the best way to maintain your culture, and it's also the most motivating for people that are within the business. If they know that all the top jobs are filled by people recruited externally, they have a glass ceiling to their career and it's not very motivational. (Looking back, I think that for a while we leaned too heavily on external hires.) Here's a great example of the value of promoting from within: Kevin Rountree joined Games Workshop as an accountant twenty-five years ago, rising through the ranks before becoming chief executive in 2015. Under his leadership, revenues at the company, which makes and sells the Warhammer fantasy war-game figurines, recently exceeded £450 million, and in the past five years, its shares have risen almost 115 per cent. And never underestimate the 'boomerang hire'. Steve Jobs returned to Apple a better leader after pursuing success elsewhere, and subsequently turned the company into a $100 billion behemoth. As mentioned earlier, at HomeServe we run an alumni club to keep in touch with those we regret losing, just in case we are ever in a position to rehire them. Don't ignore non-executive members of your board, either. Roger Whiteside was a non-exec at Greggs for five years before being asked to become chief executive in 2013. It was an inspired decision, as his strategy – focusing on food-to-go, particularly in travel locations – led to revenues doubling to £1.5 billion and a fivefold increase in its share price.

If you don't already know the perfect candidate and need to hire externally, stay clear of job-hoppers – those who have moved companies every two or three years. They may talk a good talk at the interview, but you'll regret it when they hop off again, having not delivered the required results. Hire a top headhunter. I've had great success with headhunters, all with different sector special-isms and their own black books filled with candidates with whom they have built close relationships. Get two firms to pitch for your business by providing sample candidates, to judge if they are on the right track. Take control of references rather than delegating them to HR or the headhunter. Have ten-minute phone conversa-tions with two people who will give you an 'off the record' honest view of the candidate.

Once you have a good selection, it's time for the interviews. I use a simple technique gleaned from Procter & Gamble: 'Has Done, Can Do, Will Do'. I focus on a candidate's past experiences and demon-strated achievements. The more detail I can get about a candidate's past, the more comfortable I am. I don't believe in hockey-stick companies that, having made steady losses, are bound to turn a profit tomorrow. I don't believe in hockey-stick people, either.

That said, how you rate a person is as much to do with your assump-tions as their abilities. That's why, as well as asking what have been their two business achievements, with data and quantification, I also ask questions that reveal a candidate's character – such as asking them about a significant achievement or adversity conquered during childhood.

Next, I look at the candidate's potential and their ability to acquire new skills. P&G have this down to a fine art, incidentally, and use online assessments to evaluate a candidate's cognitive abilities and potential.

Finally, I want to know that this person has the motivation, work ethic and cultural fit that I need. A lot of this comes back to Jim Collins's idea of a 'Level 5' leader, and it applies quite well to more junior roles. I want someone who gets my business strongly enough to apply all their energies to it, but also someone who, in interview, was perhaps not very showy, preferring to credit their colleagues for the successes they have so far achieved.

Put them through to a final interview if you are already excited about working with them. If not, keep looking. For me, that final interview is all about candidates presenting a compelling business plan for their role or business over the next five years. What are the big ideas? What resources will they require? And what timescale is needed to secure their success?

When I'm looking for a replacement or a key senior hire, only 'Level 5' leaders will do: incredibly ambitious, resilient, persistent and curious people, whose self-awareness and desire to learn mean they put the needs of others and the business above their own; who take responsibility, steer clear of political game-playing and give others credit when things are going well.

YOU KNOW WHERE YOU'RE GOING – BUT WHO'S STEERING?

Entrepreneurs and leaders often tell me that one of their biggest regrets – and it's one I share – is that they didn't move more decisively in getting in the right talent, or releasing the wrong recruits, soon enough. 'Go after the cream of the cream,' said Steve Jobs, Apple's much-missed leader. He understood what accelerates business growth: 'A small team of A-plus players can run circles round a giant team of B and C players.' Simon Arora echoes this sentiment: 'When I was working at 3i, one of the things I learned from the venture capital people was that it's better to back strong managers in a mediocre business model than it is to back mediocre managers in an excellent business model.' I imagine he's thinking of people like Zillah Byng-Thorne, Auto Trader's former finance chief. When the publisher

Future hired her to become its chief executive in 2014, few predicted she would transform the company into one of the UK's most valuable media assets. When she took over, the shares languished at 78p. In September 2022, when she announced that she was stepping down, they were about £16.50, and the company's estimated annual profits topped £270 million.

Another recent survey from McKinsey found that high performers are four times more productive than average ones, while high performers in complex corporate decision-making roles – the 5 per cent who deliver 95 per cent of the company's value – are an incredible eight times more productive.[*]

Due to the outsized impact a star performer can have, whenever I meet or hear about someone who impresses me, I write their names in my little black book. I might not have the right role for them at that moment, but I will one day. That is how I found Jonathan King, my first successor. 'I had various jobs at Boots,' recalls Jonathan, 'The most high profile being in international development. We were opening Boots stores overseas, and I remember we opened a store in Tokyo in a joint venture with Mitsubishi Corporation, which by a happy accident – well, not quite an accident; I called them up – is HomeServe's joint venture partner now, as we develop in Japan. Anyway, I was a mid-ranking executive in a big retail business, doing a cool job that involved a lot of travelling, it was fun, and I was having a good time.

'And all that time, just around the corner from where I lived, in the same private housing estate, there was Richard, living there with his wife Kate because (went the joke) Nottingham was equally inconvenient for both of them! Richard and I had a mutual friend, Sara Hughes, and around about February or March of 2000 she invited us

* McKinsey & Company (2017) 'Attracting and retaining the right talent', 24 November. Available online at www.mckinsey.com/capabilities/people-and-organizational-performance/our-insights/attracting-and-retaining-the-right-talent. This survey draws heavily on Hunter, J.E., Schmidt, F.L. and Judiesch, M.K. (1990) 'Individual differences in output variability as a function of job complexity', *Journal of Applied Psychology*, 75(1), 28–42.

both to her fortieth birthday party. [Richard and I] got talking, and Richard told me about his joint venture with South Staffordshire Water. He described it at the time as being a bit like "the AA for your home". Even before he told me about his aeroplane, I was thinking to myself, "Good grief, you're doing well." (In those days you could measure the success of Richard's companies by what plane he was flying. At this point it was a rather little propellor-driven affair.)

'We chatted, exchanged details, and then Richard called and suggested I come and work for him. It was a well-timed approach because I was getting just a shade bored where I was. Boots was – I assume still is – a lovely company to work for, but my personality and work style were better suited to a more entrepreneurial business. I just wasn't a retail person. Retail executives are very particular people. They *love* shopping. I wasn't into it. I couldn't look at a shampoo display and spend twenty minutes discussing why this product should be on this shelf and that product on that one.

'A while passed between our meeting and when Richard made me an offer. He jokes that I was too expensive, and he had to wait until the business could afford me [It's true: it took me six months to find enough money in the business to hire him], but one thing led to another, and I thought, "I'll try working at this strange little outfit. If it doesn't work out, I can always go back to a big corporate."

'During the interview process Richard introduced me to some of the other people he'd recruited, and I was surprised to discover a lot of them had blue-chip backgrounds. Surprised and reassured: people smarter than me had already been willing to throw in their lot with Richard. I joined in October 2000. Lots of people thought I was mad. Years later, even when we were listed on the FTSE 250, former Boots colleagues would say, "Are you still working for the water board, then?"'

Jonathan joined HomeServe as business development director. I wanted to do a deal in France, and Veolia was the front runner. They owned Générale des Eaux, France's biggest water company, and had a minority share in South Staffordshire Water. Jonathan had lived and worked in France and his French was reasonable, so he spent much of his first few months going back and forth to negotiate the venture. 'I remember asking Richard if I could use his aeroplane to go to Paris,' says Jonathan. 'He said yes, but what he didn't tell me was how tight the budget was, so instead of landing at Charles de Gaulle, the pilot and I found ourselves taxiing around a tiny airfield out in the sticks somewhere. By the time I got to Paris I realised I didn't have enough money for the taxi back to the airfield, and no means of getting any either. I decided to give the taxi driver the bad news only when we got to the airfield. I swear I hit upon Paris's nicest cabbie.'

Jonathan and I operated in the leanest, fastest way we could. On one occasion, we arrived in Lyon one Christmas Eve without TGV tickets to Paris, leapt on the train, screamed, begged and blagged two tickets from the guard, had our meeting with Veolia in Paris, leapt on the train again and amended our draft contract in the buffet car, using Jonathan's rudimentary laptop connected to his brick of a mobile phone. It was a most chaotic day, and yet we somehow impressed the Veolia board with our chromed efficiency. 'This was the first thing I noticed about HomeServe,' says Jonathan. 'Not the comical accidents that attend all young businesses, but the speed at which things got done.'

Jonathan has a theory about standard units of time in businesses. 'At Boots, nobody expected anything to get done in less than a week. At HomeServe, the standard unit of time was five minutes. Of course, that doesn't mean everything actually gets done in five minutes. But the presumption was that, after five minutes, you'd be clearly ahead of where you were five minutes ago.'

Eventually you will meet your match: the person who can replace you. It took me only a year to decide to appoint Jonathan managing director of HomeServe UK Membership – back in 2001, when we were only a UK membership business. Jonathan remembers: 'I was surprised, but I knew Richard well enough to know he wouldn't be hands-off, and this was great for me as I still had a lot to learn. The number one thing Richard hates is lack of action. He wants stuff done. If you're doing things in a halfway-sensible fashion, he'll leave you alone. If the wheels come off, he'll be forensic about working out what went wrong, and about learning lessons. Then you're off again: no harm, no foul. It's not everyone's style, but I have a natural tendency towards action and found Richard easy to work with.'

I remained as Group CEO, overseeing the overall strategy and direction of HomeServe, including its international expansion, and I still felt very much in control of the company. But I could already see where things were heading, and should be heading, for the good of the business. It had taken me eight years to gather enough courage to hand over the reins to Jonathan. I probably should have acted earlier. HomeServe had been incredibly successful, the balance sheet was healthy and the team was firing on all cylinders, but we needed to keep building and uncovering new opportunities, and I couldn't do that while I was working so hard running the UK business.

Even so, when you make big leadership team appointments, or take on any significant new hire, it's still essential to establish clear goals and expectations from the outset. This doesn't mean micro-managing. Rather, it's about giving my leaders autonomy and the space to execute their vision. With new CEOs, like Checkatrade's Jambu Palaniappan, I share a 'Working Together' document outlining my vision for the relationship, what our expectations should be and how we can best support each other's success. This sets the stage for a strong and effective working partnership.

I have learned the importance of this lesson the hard way. I once hired an excellent leader and left him alone to do his thing, gave him next to no guidance regarding our business culture and set him some wrong goals. By that one decision, I managed to put a dent in his career, and later – through a chain of circumstances, and after he had already left – I found that I had nearly destroyed the company.

Having established that A-listers are essential, let me now explain why you still have to manage them.

IT'S A BUSINESS, NOT A TALENT SHOW

In 2007, I brought in Jon Florsheim as CEO of HomeServe UK. I told him we wanted to see a boost in our membership figures. By every metric Jon was ideal for the role. He'd previously worked for BSkyB as their chief marketing officer and as managing director of their customer group. It was his strategy that grew Sky TV's subscription service.

So, it was a puzzle to us all when our customer growth started to falter. Suddenly we were getting fewer than 100,000 new customers a year, compared to an average of over 300,000 new customers in the previous three years. It turned out that Jon, a man of considerable ability, was nonetheless an awkward fit for the culture of HomeServe, and I had done nothing to ease the transition or even spot the problem.

We had a specific culture – which I clearly hadn't communicated – and Jon Florsheim was a marketing guy through and through, used to working at Sky TV. He wanted to make his bailiwick a proper marketing division. He wanted us to get into TV advertising. He didn't want to waste his time on direct mail. He also had a management style that got people competing with each other and was very financially motivated.

The team Jon put together did exactly what Jon's teams had done in the past, and to some acclaim: it focused on outbound telesales and cross-selling to an existing customer base. Both strategies work very well in the world of cable TV, but neither strategy was suited to our business. In fact, these winning strategies were exasperating our existing customers and alienating potential new ones.

The other day I came across a few very generous lines from Jon about his experience at HomeServe. I don't mind admitting they stopped me in my tracks. Here he is, singing our praises, and yet, between the lines, it's painfully clear just how ill-suited we were. 'I've worked for some interesting bosses. I know Alan Sugar reasonably well and Sam Chisholm, whom I worked for at Sky, is pretty aggressive. But there's no aggression in Richard. He may get quietly frustrated, but I've never seen him bang the table, ever. A company like Sky is driven by fairly dictatorial people that drove grown men to tears at times.'

Jon, who learned to do prize-winning business in that culture, brought some of it to HomeServe. Of course he did – we hired him, we didn't reprogram him. But cultural changes can snowball. Bit by bit, while Jon was with us and after he left, the business of HomeServe UK became less about teamwork and more about targets. HomeServe had always been a customer-centred business; that was its great strength. Now some of that customer focus was lost, as UK staff became preoccupied with the latest sales targets. When at last the penny dropped, I went to the board to say that the UK business needed a change of leadership. Jon left, and Jonathan King returned from running HomeServe USA to replace him.

Our long-serving company secretary Anna Maughan, who was witness to the whole sorry business, has this to say: 'When you look back – and isn't hindsight a wonderful thing? – you can see easily enough that we had handed Jon a poisoned chalice. As a company, we were years older than our industry regulator, the FSA [Financial Services Authority; it transitioned to become the Financial Conduct Authority in 2013]. Because we were older, and had fundamentally shaped our sector, we thought we knew everything there was to know and weren't paying proper attention to the FSA's regulations. Then, to cap it off, we hired a man who had no regulatory experience and told him to accelerate business as usual!'

That's how, rather late in the game, I learned one of my most valuable business lessons: don't hesitate to let the wrong people go – and sooner rather than later. This makes me sound like Lord Sugar on *The Apprentice*, so let me explain. Even the best of us cannot expect to fit well into every situation we find ourselves in. And if a hire or an appointment has gone wrong, the only person who can see that the fit is bad is *me*, the person hiring. I'm the only one in that situation with information enough to make a good decision. And so – and more often now than formerly – I make it. I'm as calm as I can be, and as constructive as possible. No one's asking me to enjoy this, and I don't. But no one, in the final analysis, will criticise me for doing the right thing for my business.

The people around me have noticed this change in me. I was talking with Simon Blunt for this book when he dropped this on me: 'I remember you telling me on a skiing holiday that you were planning to get rid of someone quite senior because he wasn't challenging you enough. You can be quite ruthless.' Am I? To be successful, and for the business to be successful, I have to get the right people into the business.

Simon Arora agrees. 'You can't go from a chain of twenty-one stores to a FTSE 100 company with all the same people. Different skills are required at each stage. At a senior level, the turnover is less about criticism of individuals as about who has the skills you need to deploy in that moment. We found ourselves turning over executive roles every five years or so, just to keep up with a changing business. In an ideal world, all those departures would be mutually beneficial. A store operations director who's taken us as far as he can go will likely thrive as managing director of another, smaller business. Well, that's what you hope for.'

Victoria Lynch focuses on current needs and tries not to second-guess herself. 'I often wish I had hired certain key people sooner, but then I think back and I realise, those roles would be different then to what I need now. And even if I had made those key hires sooner, and they had worked out, the Covid pandemic would have still disrupted our plans. Timing is everything, you just have to adapt to circumstances.'

Ben Francis of Gymshark deserves the last word here: 'Every individual has to grow at least as fast as the business and, all too often, problems arise that have nothing to do with the worth of the individual. They're simply to do with the speed of change in the business. I remember, our former, much-respected chief commercial officer only had digital experience – and all of a sudden we needed someone with experience in digital, retail, wholesale, new market, global . . . Someone who's only worked in e-commerce can't possibly gain that extra understanding quickly enough, and it's down to me to decide whether to back them, and put the business at risk, or bring someone else in.'

After a pause, Ben added: 'This, without question, is the least enjoyable part of my job.'

DON'T LET THE DOOR HIT YOU ON THE WAY OUT

An orderly succession can require years of planning. It's the kind of work you see being done at J.P. Morgan, where the bank's chief executive, Jamie Dimon, has identified five leading candidates to take over when he steps aside.

A *Harvard Business Review* analysis a few years ago estimated that the power vacuums, drift and poor decision-making caused by bad chief executive successions wiped out $1 trillion in market value from the S&P 500 in a year, while investor returns could be 25 per cent higher with good plans.[*]

On the other hand, there are plenty of examples of great succession work. Within a couple of years of returning to Apple as chief executive in 1997, Steve Jobs hired Tim Cook to work alongside him in various roles, handing over the reins to his protégé shortly before he died in 2011. Cook, in turn, has laid out a well-planned succession.

Britain's companies should watch and learn. A recent Deloitte report found that only 54 per cent of FTSE 350 companies had a written succession plan for the board.[†] My advice to chief executives is to start planning your succession three years ahead. You need to give your chosen candidates a challenging series of roles to see what they're made of. Not only do you want them to develop skills and deepen their knowledge about the business, but you also want to assess their character. Often, it's only by seeing how they behave out in the field that you can tell if they're an ego-free team player or a political power player. And take it from me: you want to hire the former, not the latter.

Succession planning should never be done behind closed doors. If it's open and promoted as business-critical, your teams will see the

---

[*] Fernández-Aráoz, C., Nagel, G. and Green, C. (2021) 'The high cost of poor succession planning', *Harvard Business Review*, May–June.

[†] Deloitte (2024) 'Fortune/Deloitte CEO pulse survey'. Available online at www2.deloitte.com/content/dam/Deloitte/us/Documents/us-fortune-ceo-pulse-survey-fall-2024.pdf.

opportunities that come with it. It's motivating for staff and executive teams to know that their organisation wants to encourage staff to look for the next step up. And, if you do manage to hire for the role internally, you'll need to start thinking about who will take their place and when.

Years of research conducted by the business management expert Jim Collins showed that the best-performing companies were the ones that had well-established systems for training, retaining and promoting insiders. 'It's not the quality of leadership that matters,' he says, so much as the 'continuity of quality leadership that preserves the core values and purpose of the institution while simultaneously stimulating progress into the future'.[*]

Getting the timing right on your succession plan means being honest with yourself about how long you want to be the boss. Don't just stay in the job because you can; have the humility to know when you can't give it your all. I've been so committed and passionate about my businesses that, at times, I've found it hard to confront succession planning. The buzz you get from being both founder and chief executive is incredibly addictive, and there were moments when I should have been looking to the long term, beginning the transition sooner than I did.

Finding your own replacement as CEO is particularly painful, not just for personal reasons, but because continuity counts. The average tenure of a chief executive in the S&P 500 index of top American firms is 4.8 years, slightly below the 5.4 years for the FTSE 100 – yet a study for the *Harvard Business Review* found the hundred best-performing bosses in America had been in the job for an average of seventeen years.[†] Simon Wolfson has been in charge of Next since 2001. That makes him the longest-serving chief executive of a FTSE 100 company.

[*] Collins, J. and Porras, J.I. (1994) 'Companies need not hire outside CEOs to stimulate fundamental change', Jim Collins Articles. Available online at www.jimcollins.com/article_topics/articles/companies-need-not-hire.html.
[†] HBR Editors (2016) 'The best-performing CEOs in the world', *Harvard Business Review*, November. Available online at https://hbr.org/2016/11/the-best-performing-ceos-in-the-world.

Still, I've come across great examples of young leaders who real-ised, very early on, that their best contributions to their company would be made far from the CEO's desk. They stepped down early, not to do less, but to do more. It's crucial for the founder to stay on to help direct strategy. Passenger, in which I'm invested, has retained its original founders while appointing an experienced chief executive and chairman to accelerate growth. Ben Francis founded Gymshark a decade ago, appointed his successor three years later and is still there, as committed as ever. I talked to Ben and his successor, Steve Hewitt, a veteran of Reebok, about this experience. 'Taking on Steve Hewitt as our CEO, just three years into the business, felt more natu-ral and went much more smoothly than people assume,' Ben says. (It was a good business decision, too: five years later Gymshark was worth £1 billion.) 'Steve was coming in one a day a week as an outside consultant, then two days week; by the time we were thinking of upping that to three days a week, we realised there was absolutely no point in delaying things any further. Steve came in as a full-time consultant – a sort of "CEO-lite" and not long after officially became Gymshark's CEO. It was great for me. I could concentrate on areas I was good at, like brand, marketing and product. It also meant I could work on my weaknesses and fail without consequence. I could mess up in finance, and Steve would be there to fix it. It was like being able to retake your exams until you got the grade you wanted.'

Steve Hewitt remembers, 'Ben was about nineteen months in to growing Gymshark when I got to meet both him and Lewis Morgan, Gymshark's co-founder, in the early part of 2013. My background was in growing more traditional sports brands: I'd been helping to build Reebok in Europe. The guys at the time employed about seven people, but they knew full well they were onto something: annual net sales in their business that year were around £400,000. Their biggest chal-lenge was their age. Their youth got in the way of their credibility. Age is less of an issue now than it was; maybe I'm feeling my age here, but it sometimes feels as though the younger you are now, the more back-ing you get. A decade ago, youth was a problem. And this was a shame, since youth was Gymshark's USP. The guys were building what I would call the new era of brand. Back then, most consumer goods businesses were relying on retailers and distributors to build their product range. Building your brand meant putting your goods into as many stores as possible. Ben and Lewis were looking elsewhere, towards social media, which was not very highly developed at that time. Instagram was still finding its feet. YouTube was the main player, and when they set up Gymshark, the lads used YouTube to create and build a fitness community online. They were true pioneers. They realised they didn't need to sell to retailers so long as they managed to sell through social community, on digital platforms like Shopify. They developed a cult following. The challenge they had – which is where I came in – was that suppliers in the Far East just wouldn't take twenty-year-olds seriously. What am I saying? Their bank wouldn't take them seriously! And if I'm brutally honest, I could see why. They were as cocky as hell. They were riding a wave of success and wanted everyone to know it. "Look at our £1 million business!"

'My job was to professionalise the organisation, and that involved quite a bit of kicking and screaming. Ben and Lewis knew they needed to do this, but it went against the grain: here they were, driving this sleek speedboat, and here I am trying to fit them out like an oil tanker. I remember sitting them down and saying to them, "Look, do you want to become the biggest fitness brand in Bromsgrove, or do you want to become a true global player?" They said they wanted to go global. "Right," I said, "so your answer to that question has defined where we go next." My job was to convince them that they needed a team who were smarter than they were. Trying to sell that idea to twenty-year-olds, whose every touch has turned stuff to gold, was a job of work. But then we brought in two executives who were smarter than the lot of us, they demonstrated their worth and Ben and Lewis knew a good thing when it landed in their laps: "Actually, that worked . . ."'

Steve continues: 'We went from a small pioneering social-media lifestyle brand, turning over half a million, to a company turning over £800,000, to £2.5 million, to £12 million, to £40 million, to £100 million in sales over three or four years. Our growth rate was just ridiculous.

'At this point everyone stopped talking about waves and trends and surfing success; we started talking about "building the house". Ben and Lewis had built this beautiful roof and added loft conversions and laid out the garden and so on; my job was to see to the foundations. We got to a point where everything we did was for the long term. We wanted the brand to outlive generations, not just make a quick buck.'

The acid test for their new resolve came in November 2015. 'We had built this awesome community,' says Hewitt, 'but we hadn't realised that our cult following had grown so quickly – and when you've got ten million followers on social media, you have to sometimes pivot really quickly. In 2015, we trailed our Black Friday sale a week in advance, and on the last day in November, at 7 p.m. precisely, hundreds of thousands of people across the world all landed on our website at the same time. The tech platform that we sat on was not stable enough, and the clocks were still reading 7 p.m. when the entire system went down. Many people couldn't even access the site. Others were ordering but couldn't reach the payment gateway. We got punished for that, because in those cases we ended up sending product out for free. But then, as if to make up for this, we managed to charge people for goods they never received.

'It took us months to recover. We were still dealing with the repercussions in April 2016. We wrote to every customer. I remember Ben sitting for hours, writing out letters of apology by hand. I reckon we lost the trust of 80 per cent of our customer base that day. And when your community are like football fans, totally obsessed with the team they love, then you have to accept that they will turn on you in a second when things go wrong.

'That was, I think, the moment Ben and Lewis truly understood what I'd been talking about: that it's all about the planning. You can pray for the best, but you have to plan for the worst. You need a plan C as well as a plan B. It was a defining moment that helped professionalise the organisation, and without it I'm not sure Gymshark would be where it is today. It would certainly have taken us a lot longer to get where we are now.'

THE LONG GOODBYE

The longer the founder stays on as CEO, the harder they're going to find it to leave. One of the most impressive moves Craig Waddington has made in an extraordinary career (you'll remember he built a second business when the first was snatched away from him) was stepping away as CEO of Easy Bathrooms after twelve extraordinarily successful years.

It was the company's very success that persuaded him to move on: '142 stores in, the expansion of the business has convinced me I'm just never going to be an office person. I'm much better off – and the company is better off – if I'm scouting locations, talking to local businesses and getting the measure of a place and its potential.

'I brought in Adrian Burleton as our CEO four months ago, and it's already made a difference, because it's given everyone someone to report to. When you grow from three staff to eight hundred, there can be a bit of politicking between departments. The whole leadership team is learning; this is the biggest business any of us have worked in. Adrian's the only one of us who doesn't think we're huge. He's the only one in the company who's worked at bigger companies, and he can bring us fresh ideas and insights as we grow.

'My main role now is product development. I visit China at least twice a year – I've visited over ninety times now. If I'm in the office, the business isn't moving forward. I'd much rather be out of the office, looking for the next opportunity, looking for how I can grow the business.'

Sometimes the founder just wants to leave. They've done what they can and they want to go and do something else. Their decision to leave is not particularly angst-ridden – it's more a practical matter of who will look after their baby best when they're gone. Far from clinging jealously to the reins of power, they're working hard to convince the right candidate to assume power.

This is Simon Blunt's experience, anyway. As part of the deal that brought the Mortgage Advice Bureau half a million pounds' worth of new business, its investor, Legal & General, put two of its own staff into the company. This accelerated the operation, and the relationship between company and investor developed nicely. Eventually L&G approached Simon and said, 'We've got this director who's really good at telling businesses how they can perform better. Would you like to see him?' This was Peter Brodnicki, and Simon remembers, 'He wrote this brilliant report about what we should be doing. I remember looking at my business partner at the time and saying, "This is brilliant. But how on earth do we do this?"' Reading that report, Simon and his business partner knew straight away that they were out of their depth, so they did the obvious thing – they poached Peter from Legal & General. This did not go down well. 'I remember one well-placed chap – L&G's managing director sat up straight whenever he walked in the room – he took me aside and said, "Right, then. You've got your golden goose. Don't take the mickey."'

Peter, who still felt a bit of a newcomer, was initially reluctant to take on leadership of the company, but eventually Simon managed to persuade him to organise a management buyout. 'He then took the company to great heights. I stayed invested in the company, and along with the other shareholders I made a huge amount of money,' Simon remembers. This is as well, because the sale still sticks in Simon's craw: 'We thought Peter could take the Mortgage Advice Bureau to a £100 million business and did our deal based on that. Instead, he took it to a half-a-billion-pound business. I'd had no idea just how good he really was. If I'd known, I would have negotiated harder.'

It often happens that entrepreneurs only get round to thinking about selling when things aren't going well, or when a potential buyer leaps upon their business. Both situations will limit your ultimate financial success. The trick is to lay the groundwork long before you plan to sell. Do now all that you can to be exit-ready – and you'll avoid many a sleepless night.

I should have had a plan in place. Instead, I delayed and delayed. And then, in 2022, and even as we were starting internal board discussions about breaking up HomeServe into three standalone entities, we were suddenly confronted with an unprompted offer by Brookfield Asset Management.

Collaboration is a key part of your exit strategy. You and your leadership team need to get your business on the radar by holding informal meetings with potential buyers a few years ahead of a potential sale, so that when the time comes, they approach you with a serious offer. Ask the entire team if they aim to stay with the business. Build a comprehensive growth and retention plan, which properly maps out a future transition, perhaps with a bonus structure. And if there are potential conflicts of interest, get these on the table as soon as possible. If your finance chief isn't properly equipped to deal with an exit – which is often the case in generational family businesses – bring in an adviser early. They may start pro bono, with eventual remuneration tied to the exit deal. Anticipate potential buyers' concerns, be prepared to answer their questions, have accurate figures about the worth of your business. And, finally, make sure the buyer's story about how they'll grow the business is a convincing one. It's your baby, remember.

FAMILY VALUES

There's one kind of business I've left till last because it's something of a special case. You don't have to be a fan of the TV series *Succession* to realise that family businesses have unique strengths and unique weaknesses, and many of these revolve around how the business is passed on.

I think Simon Arora must have got an early look at the scripts for *Succession*; in any event, the family has sold down and divested of B&M, the business that made their fortune. 'My brothers and I have always been very clear that we did not see B&M as a multigenerational business,' Simon explains. 'We did not want to create a situation in which eight, nine, ten cousins are fighting like cats in a sack about who gets which job and how much they're paid. The strength of our family relationships is way too important to risk in that way.'

Indeed, there is a lot that family businesses need to learn from companies that answer to shareholders. Power is best not kept in the hands of the few. Good decisions are almost always arrived at by a management team that understands the market. Many family businesses never achieve the growth they deserve; heart and head, emotions and finances, do not make for easy bedfellows and they prevent fast decision-making.

And yet Britain's corporate giants could learn a lot from how successful family businesses are run: they focus on long-term goals rather than short-term results; their profits don't come at the expense of deeply held values; and I've noticed that mistakes are more often seen as learning rather than sacking opportunities, with staff being given chances to develop. A recent study by the professional services firm PwC suggested that the family firms sector contributed £225 billion in taxes in 2021, far exceeding most other kinds of business.[*]

There are, broadly, four kinds of family firm. First, those that endure by growing, adapting and flourishing, embracing risk and consistently reinvesting. Second, those that stagnate because decision-making is too slow and dividends take precedence over investment. Third, those that are public but whose majority holding is owned by the family. Finally, there are those that implode because competing interests and rivalries lead to a fatal lack of focus.

In my experience, the best family enterprises are always evolving to create long-term value. They are resilient because of their good governance structure. Decision-making is collaborative rather than simply in the hands of whoever got handed the keys. The Arora family took the family-as-business idea and ran with it. 'For the ten or twelve years that B&M was a family-owned business,' says Simon, 'we didn't have board meetings and we didn't keep minutes worth the name. My younger brothers Bobby and Robin and I would reach decisions over

---

[*] PwC for the IFB Research Foundation (2023) 'Total tax contribution of UK family businesses'. Available online at www.pwc.co.uk/private-business-private-clients/total-tax-contribution-of-uk-family-businesses.pdf.

the kitchen table, or in snatched conversations with one of the executive committee in a corridor.'

Simon's brother Bobby was the group's trading director, responsible for products, quantities and prices, and his expertise in sourcing products meant that Simon could focus on other things, in particular finding sites for new B&M shops. 'I suppose I was CEO,' Simon muses. 'That was my nominal job title, anyway. But unlike a typical CEO, I never felt much call to involve myself in my brothers' affairs. I left our trading entirely to Bobby because I knew that, in him, I had a world-class operator for that function.'

Great family firms also benefit from a distinctive and unifying set of values running through the generations. Good examples include Iceland, run by Richard Walker after taking over from his father Sir Malcolm; Timpson, which passed from Sir John to Lord James; and Barbour clothing, where Helen Barbour is the fifth generation of her family helping to run the company.

There are also plenty of examples of children transforming the smaller businesses of their parents. Since he took over the family firm in 1975, Lord (Anthony) Bamford at JCB has grown the construction equipment company into one that employs about 18,000 around the world and, in 2022, reported a record turnover of £4.4 billion.

Unfortunately, far more medium-sized private family businesses (typically employing 15–250 workers) struggle to grow because they lack the inclination and ability. The best leaders and owners are those who, recognising weaknesses and blind spots, bring in outsiders with different skills and experiences. Of course, it's critical that these incomers are made to feel like 'part of the family', rather than being sidelined by infighting and indecision. Family members should earn the right to run the company by putting in the hard yards. They have to prove themselves as they rise through the ranks – sometimes to a greater degree than an outsider. It's very easy for family leaders to resist innovation and to make decisions that serve their personal interests. Outside leadership can reinvigorate the business and provide much-needed vision and clarity. The Wates family have brought in a series of successful chiefs to run the building contractor that carries their name.

And, if you no longer have that emotional connection to build something sustainable and prove yourself every day, then it might, after all, be time to cash out. Don't sit on a great family business and allow it to tread water. Sell, put the wealth to better use and let someone else acquire, run and grow it. Or be proactive and split it up, so that different family members can take the bits they want. This can create focus and renewed growth.

Alternatively, think about bringing in an outside investor to take a minority stake and bring capital for growth and some additional expertise, perspective and balance. Reinvestment reaps long-term dividends; you can never win by drifting.

SUMMING UP

Let it go

We're not superhuman. So why not embrace the fact that you're not God's chosen solution to every problem and hire people smarter than yourself? Life and work become infinitely more interesting that way, and you'll be able to focus on strategy rather than daily operations. As your business scales, you'll still need constant vigilance to ensure your company preserves its values. So be ready: putting the business's wellbeing first sometimes means making difficult personnel decisions.

In the end, if all goes well, the person you'll find yourself removing from their leading role in your business is yourself. Congratulations! You made something bigger than you are. Now, let it go.

You are not your business

Avoid the obsession with leaving a personal legacy. Understand that the business is about more than you and that your employees contribute significantly to its success.

Hire for succession

Seek out people who have the potential to take your place. Focus on traits like ambition, resilience and the desire to learn. Prioritise past performance and establish clear expectations. Hire based on proven success in previous roles, and set clear goals from the beginning. Offer autonomy and support to help new leaders succeed.

Don't hesitate to let a bad hire go

If a hire or appointment proves to be a bad fit, make the difficult but necessary decision quickly. In the long run this is better for everyone.

Chapter Six

Go Global with Locals

Here's the thing about global expansion: most business activity takes place in regional blocks, not in a single global market. In a part of the world you're unfamiliar with, you need to find the right leader to make a success of your business model there. You need to keep a tight grip on the business – ideally, a personal grip – for the first year. But then you'll need to loosen your grip on the reins. In the end, you'll almost certainly need to hand that business over to a local, and don't leave it too long to do that.

Charge at an unfamiliar market like a bull at a gate, and every opportunity will morph into a problem, so be aware of cultural differences before embarking on any campaign abroad. (In my experience, for instance, direct mail works brilliantly in the US and France but fails miserably in Spain and Italy.) Do your research early and thoroughly, and try to see exactly where the differences and similarities lie between your current business and your new one.

All of this golden advice can be summed up neatly in the following sentence: 'Don't do what I did.'

'We had several adventures,' says Barry Gibson, HomeServe's long-suffering chairman from 2010 until 2021, 'and because we weren't paying sufficient attention to the cultural differences that existed between our home market and these other markets, those adventures rarely led to good outcomes.' Happily for us, our successes, especially in France and the US, ended up far outweighing the failures, to the point of accelerating and transforming our entire operation. But I'll share the bad along with the good. The lessons I have to offer will be sharper that way – and, be honest, who doesn't like seeing someone slip on a banana skin?

THEY DO THINGS DIFFERENTLY THERE

The hero of our first major overseas expansion story is Rachael Hughes. I like to think of her as our former head of HomeServe's Continental European operations. Rachael is rather more down to earth, describing her job as 'trying to hold Richard back a little bit, with one arm stretched backwards as I try to pull the other shareholders forwards'. I first met Rachael in the mid-1990s. I'd bought a flat in Birmingham and was travelling down from Newcastle early each Monday morning and travelling back each Friday night. Rachael, who was working for the British aerospace multinational GKN, rented a room from me. It all worked quite well because I would be off home for the weekend, leaving Rachael with the flat to herself.

I eventually lost contact with her because she went abroad to set up a GKN joint venture, and later set up businesses in Chile and Argentina. When we were considering who to get on board to help set up HomeServe's French operation, Rachael, a fluent French speaker, came immediately to mind. I tracked her down to Buenos Aires, flew her into Miami and put on quite a show, hiring a big motorboat, and even a helicopter so I could fly her around Miami and over Gloria Estefan's house. By the time Rachael got on the flight back to Buenos Aires that evening, she'd agreed to my job offer.

Rachael started in France with three people, in what we regarded as a 'torture test'. We figured if we could pull off a HomeServe operation in France, we could pull it off anywhere. Rachael found that the hurdles she encountered were greater than anything she had come across in South America. 'I never imagined French bureaucracy could be so entrenched and so all-pervasive. Administratively, it's just hard work to get anything off the ground in France. I have nothing but admiration for anyone who succeeds there.'

At the end of our first year, we had all but failed. Rachael's assessment pulls no punches: 'We did too much stuff by committee, we had too many people participating in the marketing and we lost focus too easily. We needed to concentrate on following our business model, and we needed to stop trying to please everybody else, and certainly not worry ourselves with the political interests of our utility partners. The lesson we learned is that when we attempt to enter an overseas territory, 90 per cent of our business can be pretty well identical, leaving only 10 per cent open to local adaptation.'

Rachael's persistence and courtesy were exemplary, as she navigated France's extraordinarily centralised utilities system. What made her job particularly challenging was the way big centralised French companies tended to disregard their own regional needs. At one point she went to work with the insurance giant AXA in France to provide claims handling, only to discover that AXA's French management, who had cut their teeth on motor insurance, had difficulty seeing that a plumbing repair service is fundamentally different to a car breakdown service. A fault on a Renault Clio is the same wherever the car breaks down, but the range of problems you can encounter with a water supply pipe leak will vary depending on the terrain and the environment. Meanwhile, executives from Générale des Eaux – serving 6.5 million households – effectively advised Rachael, 'If you want to do business in a way that we recognise, you're going to have to ignore what it's like to live in France.' Rachael could see that HomeServe France needed managers on the ground who understood each region, and who would treat each region autonomously – only this ran completely counter to their previous business experience.

I had persuaded Générale des Eaux – France's biggest water company – that they should do a deal with us. I was expecting them to agree to the usual five- or ten-year branding agreement, but they would only consider a joint venture. Even then it was not an easy sell. To force their hand a little, I went to see Suez-Lyonnaise, their major competitor, and this backfired badly: when we signed with Générale des Eaux, Suez copied our business model.

Then some ill luck: our first marketing campaign launched five days after the 9/11 atrocity in New York. Our mailing had already gone out by the time 9/11 happened and, funnily enough, leaflets dropping on the doormat were not anyone's priority just then; we got a response rate of less than 1 per cent.

I can't honestly say that I even liked the product we were selling – an expensive, dual-branded, all-encompassing home assistance product, when all anyone really needed was underground pipe cover, branded as a Générale des Eaux service, for a modest annual fee.

There was one ray of sunshine: our competitors, Suez, had been just as easily browbeaten by Générale des Eaux's logic, and instead of putting a rather unnecessarily large amount of money – £1 million – into their marketing, as we had, they thought they'd go one better and invest over £5 million. When it didn't work, Suez had no room for manoeuvre and decided eventually to shut down the business.

We were constantly being told that our business model wouldn't work in this new territory, and that our offer had to be a lot more complicated. Finally – and more out of desperation than insight – we decided, 'Screw it, let's go back to our original UK offering, and our original UK way of selling it.' Our second mailing, sent out over May and June 2002, featured a cartoon leaflet with water pouring out of the lawn. We also abandoned 'Domeo', our own made-up name, and branded our leaflet Générale des Eaux Services. Overnight, a failing take-up rate of 0.5 per cent shot up to nearly 2 per cent.

But our troubles still weren't over. Our partner, under its new name, Veolia, was so impressed by our success that they decided they wanted all of the business for themselves. They tried to squeeze us out of the market. They wanted us to sell to them. Well, I don't often throw my rattle out of the cradle, but in this instance I knocked over the cradle. My board had taken a cool-headed look at the numbers and reckoned it made sense for us to sell. I wasn't having it, and in the end they went along with me. I'm glad and grateful that they did: our rearguard action gave Veolia serious second thoughts, and HomeServe ended up owning the whole of the business.

DIFFERENCES RUN DEEP

Australia was an interesting experience. Whenever I come across a British business wanting to go to Australia ('It must be easier than America, right?'), I smile a slow, cool smile.

Barry Gibson reckons we sometimes went into countries without properly researching them because they ticked a lot of boxes. 'Australia, for example: it's English-speaking, so it's bound to like the kind of things we like, right? And that being the case, it's bound to love HomeServe!' It was during Jonathan King's first year as business development director, and fresh from success in France, that he suggested we try entering Australia. 'Go for it,' I said. He didn't know anyone there, so he cold-called the managing directors of Australian water companies. Amazingly, they all agreed to meet. We did a deal with South East Water in Adelaide and launched the business. So much for the good news.

'I have never come up against such open hostility to foreigners as I did in Australia,' says Jonathan. 'The unions were openly hostile about an Australian company doing a deal with a foreign company. Immediately, the whole conversation revolved around how Australian jobs were being lost to foreigners.' This was news to us. As far as we could see, we were there to *employ* Australian workers. What did they think – that we were flying people in from Walsall? And so the litany of problems began to mount. Each was manageable on its own. Travelling in a pack the way they did, they killed us.

Australia was a small market; in the entire country today there are fewer than thirty million people. And in a country that small, that spread out and that remote, very few newsworthy things happen – which is how we ended up on the nightly news, not just once, but night after night, and even found ourselves being discussed in parliament. 'I had thought our water company was privatised,' says Jonathan, 'but most of its shares were still owned by the local government. This lent our deal a political dimension that quite blindsided us.'

'We never really found out whether Australians would have taken us to their hearts,' says Barry Gibson, 'and that's because we completely misunderstood and underestimated the power of Australian trade unions. They took one look at us and saw a bunch of chancers from overseas out to drive independent Australian plumbers out of work. The fact we're the biggest employer of plumbers in the UK swayed them not a bit. They refused to work with us and effectively ran us out of town. Germany was a similar story; we didn't really get a foothold there until I was leaving the company, in 2021. German plumbers have their own chamber of commerce upholding their "Handwerkskraft". It's like a medieval guild and, like a medieval guild, it's there primarily to prevent newcomers from disrupting the existing cartel.'

Our low take-up rates in Australia were another problem. We only got moderate responses to our marketing, and it became increasingly evident that our message about the hassle of finding a reliable plumber in an emergency wasn't playing well in a society that had such a lot invested in being blue-collar. Who were we to imply that plumbers were unreliable?! In Australia, if you didn't know a good plumber (or carpenter, or mechanic), you were expected to do the job yourself.

We also made a technical mistake. It's dry in Australia, and in their hunt for water, the trees there regularly work their way into the drain lines. It's a problem wherever you go, including the UK, but in most places it's a sufficiently rare issue that we cover it in our policies. In Australia, it's different: almost everyone has to have their sewer line cleared out every year. A lot of our take-up was coming from people delighted that we were relieving them of a regular annual expense. If we were to remain viable in Australia, we'd have to withdraw this cover, and this, on top of everything else, made Australia a non-starter. The difficulties were too great for so small a market. At the same time our US business was booming, so we refocused on that.

The notion that you have to 'fail fast' has become a horrible business cliché, but that's what we did (or were persuaded to do!) in Australia, and the market thanked us for fixing our focus so promptly. The day we announced we were leaving Australia, our share price went up.

BUILD YOUR BUSINESS BY BUILDING TRUST

In 2003, I sent my UK marketing director, Jerome McManus, to Miami, Florida, to launch HomeServe's US business. One of the great things about the HomeServe model is that it doesn't take much to test: all we needed was a small office, a few people and one partner. Partnering with a US water company to provide emergency repairs insurance proved harder than we expected, but in 2003 we managed to sign a test marketing agreement with an outfit called Aqua America. The Spanish insurance company Mapfre agreed to provide claims handling, network operations and the underwriting service. They also found us office space – they operated a road assistance service in Florida, and we rented some space in their Miami office.

What we didn't know was that this office lay at the southern end of Miami airport. This was – how can I put this? – a bit of a challenge. We had a few second-hand chairs and tables, but most of the staff were sitting on boxes, trying to strike deals between the roar of jets either taking off or landing (we were on the flight path for both). The building's security guard used to fall asleep at his desk all the time, wearing his gun. Sometimes, just before drifting off, he laid his pistol on the desk. The air conditioning wasn't up to handling Miami summers, so if someone wanted to cool down, then someone else would end up getting fried. Eventually, and to everyone's secret relief, we ran out of space.

At this point we needed new blood to accelerate our expansion, so I persuaded Jonathan King to take a fairly sizeable backward step and take the reins of what was, at the time, our smallest business. Ever since, Jonathan's been dining out on all the rookie errors he made. One occurred as he was enthusiastically explaining HomeServe's brilliant scheme to the managers of a water utility company. Why was his junior colleague Myles Meehan (now HomeServe USA's SVP of public relations) kicking him under the table? It had to do with Jonathan's use of the word 'scheme', which in American English has a meaning closer to the UK English word 'scam'. 'Jonathan,' Myles begged him afterwards, 'you just can't use that word any more!'

We speak the same language as the Americans, and we think we understand America because we've been to Disneyland, we've been shopping in New York or we've visited Santa Monica. But the culture in America is completely different, and there are fifty of them. The West Coast is different to the East Coast, the south is different to the north. You need a lot of eyes on the ground in the US market. We think when we go to America that because we speak the same language, we understand each other. That's not the case. Launching into business in the States without proper cultural preparation and some local knowledge is like going into France and expecting them to welcome you with open arms when you speak English. It's never going to happen.

What you have to do is imagine things the other way round. You're sitting in Walsall or Burnley, and three smooth-talking Yanks come in and tell you about this brilliant company they've got. You'd look at them and think, 'Do you *really* know what it's like in Burnley?'

'I can remember a meeting with a water utility in Massachusetts,' Jonathan recalls, 'and this water company was literally thirty miles from the border with Connecticut. Part of my pitch was, "Look, we've already got this business working really well in Connecticut." And the guy looked me straight in the eye and said, "Well it may work in Connecticut, but it isn't going to work here." That's like saying something works in Derby but not in Leicester.'

At first Jonathan wrote off this response as a bit of parochial silliness, but the longer he spent trying to sell the HomeServe model, the more pushback he received. In the United States, consumers have local and state loyalties. Every state also has its own laws and unique regulatory framework, which you have to follow if you want to do business there. This explained why Jonathan's potential client baulked at his talk of a standard contract. Some of the smaller companies liked to negotiate and maybe get a slightly better deal than a neighbouring water utility the next county over. The idea of someone in a smart suit pulling out a standard contract from their briefcase and expecting them to just sign on the dotted line smacked of – well, a *scheme*.

I had taken us into the US expecting it to be the home of big business, and what we discovered, at least in our own sector, was a mosaic of small businesses serving local markets. Instead of a handful of large utility companies, as you have in France, or even several medium-to-large businesses, as you have in the UK, in the States we were looking at around 17,000 small water utility companies, many of them serving just a single city. Plenty of people still pump their water up from a well. On top of that, the water supply sector was more than 80 per cent state-owned. 'The US market is incredibly fragmented,' says Jonathan, 'and that starts to make sense when you remember what Europeans always forget, which is that the US is exactly what it says on the tin: fifty countries in a political union. I vividly remember a customer in Ohio complaining because we sent her a plumber from Pennsylvania.

'Insurance is regulated at the state level, so we had to deal with different regulators in every state. Rolling out a new product means doing fifty versions of that project, each tailored to the specific geographical and legal requirements of that state. Every state has different sales tax regulations, and often cities have their own taxes too. Sales tax compliance is a whole industry there. The regulations are so complicated that we made a conscious decision, in matters where no one could possibly come to harm, that we just weren't going to comply; let them catch us out and issue a fine. When every town has its own regulations, are you really going to go from one town to another, figuring out if you need a plumbing licence?'

There was an alternative open to us: the energy market in the States was nowhere near as fragmented. Jonathan remembers, 'We realised early on that we were never going to find 17,000 water companies in the US and work with them just as we worked with water companies in the UK. We needed to find a more concentrated market, and found it in the electricity and gas sectors. Pointing the HomeServe offering at these utilities was a leap of faith for us; we had tried to do deals with electricity companies in the UK and hadn't made it work.

In the US, though, some US electricity companies already ran fairly successful HomeServe-style businesses, and that gave us confidence. Our first deal was with FirstEnergy, a Top 20 electricity company, and though we do handle some water contracts, our big US partners are all in electricity and gas.'

The take-up rate from energy customers isn't as good as we're used to, but with a much larger customer base that doesn't necessarily matter. Cracking the US water market, on the other hand, meant re-examining our whole proposition from the ground up. In particular, it meant offering our services to customers in our own name, rather than through an affinity partner. This went against our whole experience up to that point. Jonathan remembers saying to his new operations director, Neil Grant, who first made the suggestion, 'That's a stupid idea. We know that when you do HomeServe branding without a partner, you are only going to get 10 per cent of the normal take-up.'

Neil patiently held his ground because, first, we had just had some quite startling success with small, publicly owned water companies in the US – customer take-up was around 15 per cent. Second, the US is a big place: 10 per cent of a 15 per cent response is still a 1.5 per cent take-up, which is perfectly respectable for a direct mail campaign. And, as Neil pointed out to his boss, delivering the coup de grâce, '1.5 per cent of a large number is, as you know, Jonathan, large.'

There are around seventy million owner-occupied households across the United States, and we managed to sell over half a million policies under our own brand – a fifth of our total US sales at the time. Once we had adjusted to addressing customers directly, we then had to find out who these customers were. Doing all our own customer research over such a huge market was a massive task, and Jonathan decided we needed some rough and immediate data, just to be getting along with. So, he did something many senior executives would never dream of doing: he went out and looked. 'We got some addresses of customers who responded in Pennsylvania and we thought, "Let's go and have a look at the houses." We drove to Pennsylvania and had a look around. Our customers tended to live in the best-kept house in what was usually a fairly ordinary neighbourhood. They didn't have a lot of money, but they were clearly very careful with their home and looked after it.' The single best indicator of being a HomeServe customer came down to the number of ornaments in the garden. 'Gnomes, little horses, toadstools, stuff like that – you could almost guarantee that would be one of ours.'

In March 2008, in the midst of gloomy predictions for the US economy and the onset of a worldwide recession, HomeServe USA signed a deal with a water company in Kentucky. Louisville, previously best known for hosting golf's Ryder Cup, had a water company with only 250,000 customers, making it an ideal test bed for HomeServe's offering. We decided to send a leaflet to everybody in the area. The leaflet looked very similar to our initial UK mailing, albeit a little more professionally designed. So, there we were, in the midst of the US economy's worst recession in recent history, inviting people to pay $60 a year for underground water pipe cover – and a staggering *11 per cent* signed up in the first mailing! It was unbelievable, the most spectacular and successful 'moonshot' HomeServe has ever undertaken. The US was pretty much the future of the world, as far as we were concerned back then, and so it's turned out: the success and size of HomeServe USA was the making of our buyout deal with Brookfield.

With such a strong start, it was pretty much inevitable that our US business would become more successful than our UK business. A market of 350 million consumers offers a bigger opportunity than a market of 60 million. The differences in the water market were certainly daunting. But once you got a handle on the scale of the challenge, dealing with those thousands of small companies was onerous only because of the paperwork. They were essentially social utilities, run for the community and without much concern for profit. Our offering was only making their lives easier.

Launching the US business in Florida had, on the other hand, been a pretty terrible decision. Never mind the aircraft taking off and landing just a few feet over our heads, the Miami workforce was lackadaisical; the culture there wasn't at all work-oriented. TV hurricane warnings were a constant distraction; they disrupted business more than actual hurricanes. And, to top it all, the rest of the US considered Florida the home of scams. In 2008, we moved the corporate office to Connecticut, which was a great move. We found excellent hires there, and for some reason Connecticut has some of the best direct-mail specialists in the business. We kept a call centre in Miami for a while, then moved it to Chattanooga, Tennessee – another good decision.

Jonathan made the decision early on to stay in the US, and even got himself a green card, which allows him to live and work there permanently. Even now, though, at the end of meetings, people sometimes say to him, 'So when are you going back to London?' They have no idea who they're up against.

If you're an incomer to the US, you'll eventually want to appoint Americans to run your operation, not so much because they 'speak the language', but because they're adept at juggling America's fifty separate cultures. 'Even then you've got to watch yourself,' says Jonathan, 'because the underlying animosity between a person in, say, Pennsylvania and a person in California can reach a level where each would sooner talk to a Brit!

'The trick, I think, is not to rush things. In the early days you'll want to send your own people into that foreign territory, because only they can establish your business culture.' Jonathan has also found this to be true in Japan, where he's working with Mitsubishi to introduce the country to the HomeServe brand. 'I can't be there all the time, and I notice that if I'm absent for too long, the team starts to lose confidence in our odd way of doing things.'

Back in 2017, when HomeServe's board was thinking again about developing new markets, Jonathan had led a desktop exercise and Japan came out a clear winner: here was a big market with an ageing population and a recently deregulated energy sector. Jonathan was a bit startled because during a company sabbatical in 2011 he had gone to Japan and concluded it wasn't for us; back then, however, the energy companies were all publicly owned. 'I knew we couldn't break into Japan on our own,' Jonathan explains. 'It's hard enough to get deals with American utilities, let alone Japanese ones. But then I found out that Mitsubishi Corporation had been – and actually still was – a minority shareholder in South Staffordshire Water. I knew the managing director at South Staffs and asked him to introduce me. My friend at South Staffs didn't hold out much hope, but to our delight Mitsubishi were very interested to hear from us. They wanted to be more consumer-facing, and our business model fitted their strategy perfectly. We signed a joint venture agreement in January 2019, launched a year later and now have nearly a quarter of a million customers.'

It turned out that Mitsubishi remembered HomeServe from when we were part of South Staffs. They'd been following HomeServe's story ever since. I've heard that Japanese companies require quite a long-term relationship with people and an understanding of how they work before they consider a partnership. Still, I'd no idea we'd been the unwitting object of a fifteen-year courtship.

'Japan being such a risk-averse culture, it's been hard there to establish the HomeServe culture, which is predicated on trying stuff and letting it go if it doesn't work,' Jonathan observes. 'If things go wrong in an overseas operation, and they will, you need one of your own there to stand up for your ideas. Local teams who run into difficulty will quite naturally say, "This doesn't work; we'll have to change it." You need someone there to say, "Okay, it didn't work on this one occasion, but don't worry, keep going, because we know from experience this is worth persevering with." '

REMEMBER WHO YOU ARE

HomeServe USA has been certified by Great Place to Work, a global authority on workplace culture, for four consecutive years – a recognition that is based entirely on employee feedback. In 2023, HomeServe UK was recognised in the Top 50 Inspiring Workplaces in the UK and Ireland. With these plaudits and others at our back, you might assume that HomeServe must have some tremendous central 'people' function – and heaven knows, we've tried. We have recruited a few HR directors over the years to try to unify our culture. Every one of them has hit the same brick wall: our overseas MDs ring or email us with what boils down to the same complaint: 'Why are you trying to dictate our culture here? Leave us alone! We know what we're doing!'

The thing is, much of the pride that comes from working with HomeServe comes from knowing your own market inside out. So, plastering some global identity over ourselves is not just redundant; it actually runs a bit counter to who we are. If we're truly focused on the customer, then we know each market is different, and we can serve it best by playing to its particular strengths.

As Barry Gibson emphasises, local conditions will win out over grand plans every time. 'Italy's a good example. There's no especial opposition to our business, no great rival or vested interest, and yet the territory's always been a bit of a disappointment for us. Unless you really dig into what makes the Italian market tick, and unless you've got the muscle to work through those differences, foreign territories are hard work.'

One intriguing venture at HomeServe involved understanding the Spanish home insurance market. Spain, like Britain, is a land of owner-occupiers, but that's where the similarities end. Around two-thirds of Spanish homes are actually flats in a large building. You'll raise a family in them and live there for maybe twenty-five or thirty years. That flat is your number-one investment, and you're going to look after it just as carefully as any Briton looks after their house. But, as we discovered, the sort of repair cover you need is going to look quite different. There's another significant difference in the Spanish market: in Spain the contractors are not one-man bands but small companies with, say, a dozen plumbers working for them. The workers are happy where they are and, for us, contracting with a company is easier than contracting with an individual.

HomeServe's UK business is almost the outlier now because it directly employs about 760 plumbers and gas engineers. France, Spain and all the others use a network of contractors for emergencies but have their own directly employed heating installers.

In England, which is relatively urban, there's no shortage of trades wanting your custom, and our main issue, when we were using contractors, was quality. Frankly, when we hired independent contractors, too many of them produced substandard work. We experimented with employing some people directly, and we found that the best contractors were more than happy to sign on with us; for them it meant less paperwork, more security and more time spent doing the job they were skilled in.

But you don't need to relocate very far before you find you have to change your model. In Scotland, the distances can be huge and the contractors are few and far between. They know their region well, they depend on word of mouth and good relationships, so they're very trustworthy, and anyway, there's not nearly enough work to keep a staff of engineers on the payroll. So, in Scotland we use contractors to back up our network.

There's always the risk, though, that in cleverly adapting to local conditions, you throw out too much of what makes you *you*. 'You've got to keep your business model super-simple,' says Steve Hewitt. 'It's a bit like making a cake. If you change one ingredient, maybe change the colour of the icing, it doesn't affect how the cake tastes. But if you start mucking about with the core ingredients – the flour, the milk – the cake's not even going to rise, never mind taste any different. You need to keep the core ingredients of your model the same, and tweak it to local markets.'

For us that core consists of 'daring to care' – putting systems in place that allow our people to go that extra mile for customers, and so win their loyalty. It includes 'doing the right thing', which I like to think was baked in to our business long before the box-tickers arrived. In particular, we think a lot about the effect of our actions on individual communities. We're in the infrastructure game, after all, where no one is an island. Our third tenet (let's stop at three) is, 'own the problem'. For a start, the best person to fix an honest error is the person who made it. Then there's the fact that every problem can be recast as an opportunity, so long as you're prepared to look at it long and hard enough.

ENTRY WOUNDS AND HOW TO AVOID THEM

I meet many British entrepreneurs who are standing at a crossroads. With a successful product, steady growth and a loyal customer base, they want to accelerate success and expand into new geographies. Should they go it alone, investing their own assets in a new country? Or is there a role for franchising or licensing?

To begin with, I'd identify if there was a potential competitor already operating successfully in the territory I wanted to expand into. If there was: good! It proves my idea is already working and there is potential for growth. Second-mover advantage will allow me to take what's working, then adapt and improve it. Next, take a leaf out of Steve Hewitt's book (and mine, come to that), and seek countries where you have to change only 10–15 per cent of your business model. Keep the core business as is and change the minimum to be success-ful. If you need to radically change your product or business model, you really should think again about going into that country. Look at countries where your UK export sales are already highest, because they will offer a better chance of faster growth.

Going global means setting up local. You cannot maximise your international potential if you direct everything from the UK. You need a small office in-country and a smart outsourcing strategy that lets you rent warehousing and logistics skills as needed. The UK fitness clothing brand Gymshark has done this with the e-commerce logistics firm Radial to fuel its expansion in North America and Canada.

Don't delegate international development. As the founder or chief executive, you need to be on the ground doing the research, talking to potential customers, learning the culture and imparting knowledge of your business to as many people as possible. If that means hiring a chief operating officer to run your day-to-day business in your home country, do it. Then, as fast as you can, find a local mentor in your chosen country – one with insights that no amount of data can match. If they are convinced by you and your idea, they might even offer their expertise, contacts and knowledge for free.

Be prepared to invest and take profits backwards. Things take time, so be patient. Don't make any rash decisions until you have worked your socks off for twelve months, and don't run before you can walk.

When expanding into unfamiliar markets, you could also consider a joint venture, master franchise or licensing model. It's how American burger chain Five Guys has built its UK and European operation, thanks to the business-building acumen of Carphone Warehouse founder Sir Charles Dunstone. It now has about three hundred branches. Indeed, the fifty-fifty joint venture is so successful that, in some cases, Five Guys branches generate more revenue than the neighbouring McDonald's.

Under the joint venture model, instead of the franchisor directly recruiting a franchisee, an experienced third party provides the finance, finds the sites and staff, and operates the business. Their local contacts and knowledge are key to growing the business. It's a faster and lower-risk way to scale, but you will have to share the profits. This model has worked extremely well for Mansour Group, whose partnerships with General Motors, Caterpillar and McDonald's have been hugely successful in the Middle East.

The granddaddy of all franchise models is, of course, Coca-Cola – not a single company, but a network of almost three hundred independent ones connected to the vast umbrella that is the Coca-Cola Company. It owns the drink's secret ingredients but has at times sold bottling rights to partners across the world, reducing manufacturing, storage and distribution costs and remaining local while leveraging a powerful global brand.

On which subject, why is Coca-Cola a US company and not a British one? Britain has the talent, ideas, reputation and experience. What we lack, I fear, is ambition. We're limited by an old-fashioned attitude that views manufacturing success through the prism of exporting overseas goods that are made here in the UK.

Sintela, the Bristol-based remote sensors developer, is one of the UK's fastest-growing companies and made 90 per cent of its £10.4 million in sales overseas last year, in part because of the hubs it's set up in India. UK businesses need to set up subsidiaries in new countries; selling British-made goods abroad is not enough.

SUMMING UP

Growing global, thinking local

When Jonathan King went to work at HomeServe USA, he was already determined to leave the company in the hands of a predominantly American staff. 'Long term, I wanted to show our American staff that there were career paths, that you could get to a senior job without being British,' he says. 'We needed that – if you are British, you just don't know everything about America. You make rookie errors because you don't know the people, and in the end you're not a local.'

When expanding into a new market, be patient above all. Be prepared to invest and see your profits slide. Start small, testing, pivoting and figuring out the landscape. Don't run before you can walk.

Don't change too much of your model

If you need to change more than 15 per cent of your business model, this might not be the right country to go into.

Local markets matter

Big businesses operate across a mosaic of regional markets, each with its own laws, regulations and customer preferences. Adapt your approach to these local conditions.

Boots on the ground

To make informed marketing decisions, visit new markets, observe neighbourhoods and understand where your ideal customer lives.

Embrace local expertise

Understand the cultural differences and nuances of business. Hire local managers who can navigate the complexities and foster strong relationships in the new market.

Localise for growth

You can't run an international business entirely from headquarters. Setting up satellite offices or partnering with regional specialists is key to better understanding your customers and attracting top local talent.

Chapter Seven

Evolution, Not Revolution

In any new business, the atmosphere is intoxicating and your mind works twenty times faster than normal. Everywhere you look there's a different and useful way you can channel your energy. What are your business activities? Are you doing them better than the competition? Are you disrupting the market? Are you creating a new sector?

Jeremy Middleton and I managed to lose half a million pounds of South Staffs's money before we hit upon a marketing and business formula that, in just five years, built them and us a £7 million business. That was a time when I went out of my way to recruit entrepreneurs, I think because I saw a little bit of myself in them. But you need a balance in an organisation, and it took us a while to self-correct. It's as well we did, because in a regulated industry in particular, an unremittingly entrepreneurial culture can get pretty toxic: you have people coming up with great marketing ideas but not thinking in an organised way about all the other necessary aspects of the business.

In the end, assuming you're still standing after that heroic start-up phase, you start to mature. You start to focus. The war stories you gather are not quite as funny, and the carnage you leave behind pricks your conscience just that little bit more. Where once you saw opportunities in every problem, you start to see problems in every opportunity.

This is called success. You've built something, and now you need to look after it and nurse it to adulthood. In the end – and one way or another – you will have to let it go.

This is a chapter about how you can encourage your company's evolution. It's about what happens to it, and to you, after your iconoclastic heyday. It's about how you mend and nurture and transform the market your younger self disrupted.

BREATHING SPACE

Given how much practical help they gave us, it sounds a bit ungracious to say that the best thing South Staffs ever did for us was to leave us alone. But facts are facts: Jeremy and I were sales and marketing people; South Staffs Water saw that, and by bolstering our operations and by letting us do our own thing off in a corner, they let us play to our strengths.

Brian Whitty recalls: 'When I joined [South Staffs as CFO], there was a five-year plan in place which said that the water company was going to make something like £15 million in profit by the year 2000 and Home Service (as it was then known) was going to make a million. Consultants Arthur Andersen reviewed this plan and said that while the water company profits looked sensible, the Home Service forecast was hugely optimistic – it was never going to happen. That year, Home Service made about £7 million.'

By 2003, Home Service had become much bigger than South Staffs, and the difference between the two businesses had grown to be very evident indeed. South Staffs was all over the nuts and bolts of putting pipelines in and maintaining its network. Home Service was a little bit off the wall – a tail that, if we weren't careful, was going to start wagging the dog. I decided it was time to separate Home Service from its parent.

Maybe there were problems with the demerger that I've glossed over with time and hindsight. I honestly can't think of any. Our company secretary, Anna Maughan, remembers an easy and friendly transition: 'South Staffs never expected Richard to become one of them, and they never wanted to be HomeServe either. By the time we demerged in 2004, we felt like friends sharing the same space.'

We had things to divvy up, of course. We had been sharing group IT, payroll and that kind of thing. As far as which employee went where, there was never any issue: you already knew who you were working for – 'Except for me!' Anna was in an unusual situation. 'As company secretary, I was offered a job on both sides. I opted to go with HomeServe.'

South Staffs was acquired quite quickly after the demerger. Very few water companies are publicly listed any more; they're mostly in private hands because it's much more difficult in this increasingly regulated environment to make the right returns for public shareholders. South Staffs have been owned by private equity ever since, have changed owners several times and, so far as I can see, they've done very well for themselves.

Barry Gibson, a non-exec since 2004 who became our chairman in 2010, has always regarded HomeServe as a bit of a queer fish: 'a very unusual example of a big corporate organisation that grew out of a small corner of what was once a nationalised industry.' He gives me the credit for shaping a distinctive HomeServe culture from the start, so that the demerger felt natural and inevitable. (Since it's my book, I'll take those laurels.) 'The South Staffs board approached the task sensibly,' says Barry. 'They knew they would not be able to develop the business in the way that Richard wanted to develop it, because they didn't have the kind of capital Richard needed, but mainly because they didn't have, and didn't particularly want or need, to pivot to HomeServe's way of doing things. It's also worth saying that since South Staffs's shareholders received shares in the new company as well as the old, they did very well.' (This was particularly true, I remember, of Jonathan Ruffer, who I'd met many years pre-demerger with Lindsay Bury, my first chairman. He bought a significant chunk of South Staffs stock.)

MEASURING SUCCESS

Success depends on knowing what matters at each point in the four phases of the life of a business. I've talked a fair bit about starting up and proving the model, but in this chapter I'll concentrate on team expansion and growth, expanding abroad and, finally, maturation.

Whether you should concentrate on revenue, profit or cash depends on which bit of the cycle you're in. In the earliest stage, your core ambition must be to prove the business model, copying and pivoting as needs arise. There's little benefit in growing revenue massively at this point; size is less important than getting things right and minimising costs. Cash is what you need – your cash, rather than anyone else's, because bringing other people's cash into your business too early will dilute your shareholding.

Once the model is proven, though, you should definitely seek support. This is when revenue takes precedence, because you need now to prove the scalability of your business. You'll need investment to scale up, build a stronger infrastructure and hire a great management team and support staff. It takes time to get these pieces in place, and the longer you delay securing investment the more you'll be playing catch-up.

When you've got a business that can provide a healthy profit margin on sales and a significant return on your capital, then you're in the third phase, and it's time to think about adding an international dimension to your model and making it 'omnichannel'. Hitting the best balance might mean taking more of your business online or exploring the possibilities of bricks and mortar.

In all these cycles, cash remains king. Having plenty in the bank might not be your business purpose, but it enables you to grow faster and with greater certainty. High revenue from sales might look impressive, but regular inflow of cash is much more important.

It's interesting how different industries throw up different priorities. When I talked to Simon Wolfson, he raised the importance of cash, and said that if he were editing this book, he'd make it a 'tenth step' to making a billion. Simon comes from an industry where margins have to be big enough to cope with the bad years. If you look at failed retail companies, you will find that in successful years they could afford to work on very thin margins – say, around 2 per cent – but when a bad year hit (and everyone has them) their sales dropped, their margins disappeared and their fixed costs stayed up, bankrupting them. Amazon, true, has succeeded in growing on very thin margins, but only because they're obsessed to the point of neurosis by cash flow.

At some point in the development of a business, something will go wrong. So create, now, a dashboard of management information that shows you the health of your cash reserves alongside revenue and profit. Look at cash weekly and look at revenue and profit monthly. Do this, and your problems will remain troublesome, but no more than troublesome. Fail to do this, and – well, we've all seen the movie *Gremlins*.

If you're not generating cash, your business will fall over. (Think of your shareholders: it's their money you're spending, and they expect you to maintain returns on capital and margins that are high enough to fuel your growth.) Cazoo is a perfect example of a company that didn't pay enough attention to the four phases of healthy business development, preferring instead to grow internationally far too early. This online used-car business expanded across Europe without ensuring that its model worked sufficiently well in the UK. When it listed as a special-purpose acquisition company (SPAC) in New York in 2021, three years into its life, it was valued at $8 billion. But it failed to get beyond the first phase of proving the business model! Annual losses far exceeded £500 million, and it went into administration in 2024.

As you'll have gathered from the previous chapter, at HomeServe I had itchy feet, wanting to open in more territories and diversify our product range. If I had been committed to doing less but better, we would have been a bigger business and grown faster, benefiting from a higher net profit. For that reason, it's always a good idea to have a chief financial officer strong enough to give you a hard time. A good CFO keeps everyone disciplined, challenges new ideas and investments, and keeps the company's thinking focused on the core business.

So, how should you measure success?

As I said a bit earlier, business people think in numbers, not because they're maths whizzes (not at all) but because only numbers can abstract their business to the point that they can make any sense of it. The problem is that numbers are malleable. You can recast them any number of ways. Anyone who thinks figures can't lie had better not go running about with scissors. Telling the truth with figures is far harder than telling the truth in plain words. For example, say you've turned a profit: well, have you? Are you talking about your gross, your net or your operating profit margin? Are you measuring your return on assets or your return on equity? (And we haven't even mentioned EBITDA...)

Rather than get lost in the terminology, let's establish a few simple ground rules. Revenue is not the sharpest tool for measuring the health of your business. It's considered a 'vanity' metric because it doesn't take into account the cost of generating that revenue. Obviously you want revenue – growing customers and sales is vital – but the revenue figure won't tell you how much that effort is costing.

Profit can also be misleading. It's certainly a better measurement than revenue, but it won't pay the bills. You can be profitable but run out of cash if your customers take too long to pay you, or you go bust because you haven't adapted to a changing market (BlackBerry and Blockbuster are classic examples of this, Mothercare and Wilko more recent ones).

The key to wealth generation is getting the model right, and you'll know when it's right when the cash starts rolling in and not before. That's why cash is king.

What happens to people who ignore their cash flow? The ones who don't make enough cash, fail. That's simple enough. But there are others who do make enough cash, or so you would think, and yet they squander it. Rather than keep a healthy reserve, they spend it on nice-to-haves, until nice-to-haves are almost the whole of their business. It's like putting alcohol through a still – you pour it in at the top, and it goes through all these fancy new tubes and processes on the way down through the still, and when you turn the tap at the bottom, hardly anything comes out. Exactly the same can happen with cash going through a business.

DON'T LET THE PERFECT GET IN
THE WAY OF THE GOOD

Procrastination is the enemy of good business. Get comfortable with making decisions based on having only about 70 per cent of the information you'd like. If you strive for perfection, your competitor will beat you to the punch.

HomeServe is a business where things change a lot, so we look for people who are pragmatic and can roll with the punches. It's not for everyone, and I've seen a lot of people come and go over the years, and many who've left have gone on to be super-successful elsewhere. For those who 'get' HomeServe culture, it can become addictive. When our group legal counsel, Emma Thomas, first left HomeServe and went to a new organisation, she didn't know what to do with herself. She was used to much more responsibility. The change of pace when she arrived at her new job made her wonder if she'd gone and sat at the wrong desk.

I often talk about HomeServe to people as a fast company; then, sometimes, I have to correct myself, because I can see people are picturing a place gripped by perpetual crisis. That's not at all what I mean. Rather, we cultivate a sense of freedom: an ability to get things done. A large part of that is limiting the amount of bureaucracy our people have to wade through. My tendency, if I trust people, is to let them get on with things. I don't always need to be consulted.

Does this approach lead to errors? Absolutely. But, what of it? Too many of us procrastinate because we are waiting for every last bit of data to come in before we make a move. Why not make your decision early, when you're three-quarters sure of your move and you still have time to change tack if required? 'Speed is undervalued,' Jonathan King reckons. 'Taking too long to do things or make decisions can lose you a lot of competitive advantage.' When he was at Boots, the prevailing attitude was that a year spent getting from an 85 per cent good decision to a 99 per cent good decision was a year well spent.' When he came to HomeServe, he encountered a different philosophy: 'Get three-quarters of the way there and try it. If it doesn't work, we've only lost a couple of months and we can tweak it or try something else.' Apply that method, and you'll develop your business up to six times faster than Boots ever could.

Discussions of pace in business often point to the meeting schedule and suggest that you slash it. What meeting ever needs to be more than ten minutes long? Who needs PowerPoint? Who needs *chairs*? To this I would add one wrinkle: by all means have a long meeting, but if that's what you need, make sure everyone's prepared for it. I'm very uncomfortable going into a meeting if I haven't got something to read beforehand. So never mind your murder-by-PowerPoint in the middle of my meeting – give me something to read beforehand! Anna Maughan finds that this is the biggest difference between us and Brookfield. 'The HomeServe board would assemble having read every paper. Brookfield's board gets together so they can go through the papers together. It works for them, I guess, but it's not the HomeServe way.'

In my work, I expect leadership teams to meet each week to discuss critical issues that fall outside of their day-to-day responsibilities. They decide then and there to do, well, *something* – anything within reason, just so we're not carrying the same issue over to another meeting weeks later.

This attitude rang a lot of bells with the people I talked to. 'We consider speed to be an intrinsic part of B&M's competitive advantage,' says Simon Arora. 'For a growing business, a disruptive business, it's better to be fast and 80–90 per cent right than be 100 per cent right but slow.'

Give people responsibility and accountability and they will make things happen. The astonishing recent growth of HomeServe's German operation, where Thomas Rebel has overseen eleven acquisitions in three years, is proof that if you give people more responsibility, they will put the pedal to the metal. Since Brookfield acquired us, we've split the company into three, with the aim of moving faster and giving more autonomy to each business.

A GOOD BUSINESS WILL NOT LOOK AFTER ITSELF

The brand proposition for the high-street fashion giant Next is simple: give customers well-designed, high-quality products at affordable prices. But Next handles 20,000 different items! No one mind can oversee them all. The only way for such a large organisation to be nimble is to give its departments a strong degree of independence. Everything has to make a margin, it has to be great value for the customer and it needs to reflect the broader values of the company (you won't find provocative childrenswear at Next).

But that still leaves direct reports with a lot of wiggle room, and Next CEO Simon Wolfson has to rely on them to do what's best for their business. Simon can't control them in any direct way and, more than that, he knows not to. Next boasts men's, women's and kids' fashion as well as home brands. All of those markets change in different ways and at different speeds, and Simon has to have people who can respond. In those circumstances, if he's hired the wrong people, then Next's brand value will start to dissipate. I know Simon thinks this because I talked to him – and I know he's right because this is what happened to HomeServe.

I mentioned in Chapter Five how, from 2006, HomeServe UK's membership business had become less about teamwork and more about targets. By 2011 it had become quite political. I also told you that I went to the board to explain that the UK business needed a change of leadership. Here's what I didn't tell you: I was far too late, things had got worse than I thought, and HomeServe was already under scrutiny from the industry regulator. The Financial Services Authority had first started looking at the retail insurance sector around 2006. It reckoned that sales strategies needed careful monitoring by independent senior managers. By then, HomeServe had been in this business for fifteen years and had built up a great record for customer service. We thought we were doing a great job of regulating ourselves – after all, we were older than the FSA itself.

The truth of the matter was, the sales environment had changed around us, and we hadn't changed to keep up. When the regulator announced an investigation into the sales methods of the credit card insurance company CPP, it drew me up cold. What if we'd been guilty of mis-selling? Well, that was hardly likely – but still, if we had mis-sold a product, how would we know? It's the pilot's worst nightmare. You hit fog and you think you're still flying. Actually, you're falling.

I commissioned Deloitte to do an independent review of our sales culture. Its report did not make easy reading. Something horrible had happened to the culture of our membership business. Problems were staring us in the face, and we weren't picking up on them. We weren't even seeing them. I discussed things with the board, and we dragged Jonathan King back across the Atlantic to take charge of HomeServe UK a second time.

Jonathan's memories of the crisis begin somewhere in Japan: 'HomeServe had an unwritten policy that after ten years, you could take a sabbatical. I realise now that Richard knew he was about to land me with a difficult job, because he let me have nine or ten weeks off before I started. I had always wanted to travel overland from London to Japan, so I did. Then I came back to Walsall.' Tom Rusin had taken over from Jonathan in the US, leaving Jonathan free to return to the UK in the summer of 2011. It must have been a bit of a culture shock for him, after living so long in New York and spending time in Florida and Connecticut. Very soon he discovered he had bigger things to worry about. Or, as he puts it on the tape, 'The business was in a bit of a state.' It certainly was.

Jonathan did his own investigating and found our senior sales executives saying things like, 'Well that's okay, isn't it? It's only a fairly small percentage of calls where the customer isn't sure what they're buying, so we're probably within the industry norms, aren't we?' I said earlier that cultural change in a company can snowball, for good and for ill. Jonathan goes further: 'Culture beats process every time. What I found when I got back to HomeServe's membership operation was a very driven group of managers who were incredibly financially focused. They evaluated every decision by asking, "What does this mean for our bonus?" It was all about how the management team could enrich themselves. It was not remotely customer-friendly.

We'd always rewarded people well, but now there were lots of extra opportunities for self-enrichment and they were undermining our values.'

The problem was, though, there was just too much wrong. Jonathan remembers: 'I knew the FSA were coming in, but we couldn't change everything in time. I said to myself, "Right, okay, we are in real trouble here."' We were doing the wrong thing by customers. We were selling them products they didn't understand. We were cold-calling them incessantly. It was a culture – wrong for us in the first place – that went against a rising tide of consumer protection legislation. 'The FSA hated what we were doing,' Jonathan recalls, 'and the more dealings I had with them, the more I realised, they had always hated us. They didn't like our products and they didn't see the point of them. Now we had given them a cast-iron reason to go after us, and they went at it with a vengeance, determined to make an example of us – their first big retail case.'

The obvious solution would have been for us to throw some middle managers and sales agents under the bus. You know the kind of thing: 'Junior members of staff may have been overenthusiastic and broken the rules . . .' Heaven knows, we saw plenty of those kinds of excuses during the 2008 US mortgage crisis. Instead, and guided by the better angels of our nature, the board and I agreed with Jonathan: we should shut down our marketing completely. Stop all new sales, he said. Stop all outbound calls. Effectively, Jonathan told us that we would have to rebuild the business from the bottom up.

The HomeServe board helped me a lot throughout the FSA crisis, but, of course, their first loyalty had to be to the business. Not to put too fine a point on it, they had to decide whether I was the right person to go on as leader. In the end they decided that, while this was a crisis I could have foreseen and should have averted, the problem was not to do with my character. Mistakes had been made, but they were fixable, not systemic or critical to the future of the company – and the board decided I was the best person to fix them. That was gratifying, but what really moved me was their fierce defence of their decision, in the teeth of an ever-more-intense investigation. Regulators can be very cunning to get the answer they want. It was important for the board to be unified, supportive and strong, as the FSA was primed to exploit any weakness. I'm sure the regulator would have loved for me to throw in the towel and walk away. The board was determined for that not to happen.

The board at that time had about five non-executive directors and three executive directors, and they were as frenetically busy as the rest of us. The board wasn't just silently rubber-stamping in the background. It was, for example, very much a part of bringing Jonathan back from the US to fix the UK operation. Board members attended dozens of meetings – town halls, small meetings, company-wide meetings – about HomeServe's problems and how to fix them. Not only were they travelling up and down the country, talking to staff and explaining our position, they were themselves fielding a barrage of questions from the FSA.

You can imagine what happened to our share price when we announced that we were no longer selling anything. It fell by a third in one morning and went on tanking. The bears in the market reckoned, 'Right, this thing was a fairly niche business in the first place; now it's going to go bust.' But there was not just a financial cost: Anna Maughan remembers walking through the car park and finding people crying. 'The people in our call centres, our frontline staff, were mortified by that word "mis-selling". They had been going in to work every day, making every effort to serve our customers and get them the right products. When we stopped selling, they were all sent home. They didn't know what it meant for their jobs, and because the press had taken up the story, friends and family were saying to them, "Oh, you were working for that lot." People took this very personally. There's a lot of pride in the HomeServe name and organisation. We have many long-serving people. They really felt it.'

In simple terms, we'd been using retail selling techniques that are perfectly fine in an ordinary retail environment. 'Why don't you buy one of these policies? It's only a pound a month, and if you don't like it, tell us, and we'll refund you.' That seems a fair way to close a sale, doesn't it? Well. Regulation in our industry was fairly new, and

HomeServe was deemed subject to the Financial Services Authority because our product was considered quasi-insurance. We'd first come under FSA rules around 2005–2006, and frankly nobody had paid much attention. We weren't even selling insurance policies, technically: we were an agent. Our job was to fix things. This is what we told ourselves.

The FSA review forced us to think carefully about who we were and what we were doing. Essentially, the FSA said, 'You jolly well *are* selling insurance, and you can't sell an insurance product unless you understand the customer's needs and until you're sure what you're selling represents value for money. It must be something the customer needs or should have.' A simple enough rule – and we had broken it.

The FSA's 'know your customer' standard forced us to ask ourselves, 'Do we really know all our customers? Is it really enough for us to say, "If you don't like it, send it back"?' That's fine for retail, but not when we're dealing with vulnerable customers, perhaps a frail eighty-two-year-old who's already bought the very policy we are trying to sell. Other companies were sometimes bundling our services into their products, so the consumer might already have our product and not know it.

In such a crisis, Anna found Jonathan King was pivotal to the company's survival. 'He gathered the staff and said, "Look, we're in this together, and it's going to take all of us, but listen: no one in head office is casting glances out of the window. We're totally committed to sorting this out." He came into Walsall every day and walked around the offices and talked to everybody and found time for everybody. He was there all hours. He barely got any sleep. He got dragged down to Canary Wharf to be interviewed by the FSA I can't tell you how many times.'

Here's what we learned about the FSA (now the Financial Conduct Authority, FCA). They have all the power. They aspire to be the customers' champion, and they're very, very proud of the fact. They don't care a jot for your shareholders. They don't care a jot about your employees. They are not in the least bit interested in mending your business. They are there to make problems vanish, and you are the problem. 'And they are always right,' Jonathan laughs, 'except when they're very obviously wrong, so you have to pick your battles carefully.

'We did choose to fight one battle: the FSA said we had to stop auto-renewing our policies. This would have killed us, since our business model relies on renewable income. Auto-renewals are the bane of everyone's online life, of course; they're like the weed you can never get rid of. But we argued successfully that insurances are a different matter. With the appropriate notice, insurances absolutely should auto-renew, given how many people would otherwise find themselves caught out and without cover in an emergency.'

To take care of the issue, the board told Jonathan, 'Do whatever you think is necessary,' and Jonathan took them at their word. 'We laid off hundreds of people. Regulators like big gestures. Not once did I get any pushback from the board. Within a year, the entire senior management of HomeServe Membership was gone. It was best to get a new team.'

Now, how's this for irony – at the end of our first year of recovery our profits went *up*, because we weren't spending anything on marketing. Then (you're not flying; you're falling) our customer base started to shrink. 'It took us two and a half years to rebuild the company,' Jonathan remembers. 'It was an exhausting time personally, but I had the backing, so I was at least able to project some confidence.'

Jonathan's final job was to negotiate the fine that the FSA was bound to issue us, and also to consider their final notice – which is the document containing all the regulator's juiciest, most quotable judgements. Here's what happens: you get a draft, you have a month to negotiate the wording, and if you get an agreement within a month, you get a discount on the fine. It's like the parking ticket you can't quite be bothered to dispute, because they'll let you off half if you settle. Yes, exactly like a parking ticket – only for £34 million, after the discount. Subsequent fines issued to the banks Santander and NatWest, and to do with failures around money laundering, ran into the hundreds of millions. At the time, though, ours was the biggest fine for retail non-compliance the FSA had ever issued.

The board told Jonathan: 'Don't worry about the money; just worry about what the document says.' Some wag in our company had cracked a gag on our internal email about our customers not being sensitive to price. The FSA wanted that in, verbatim, but Jonathan wasn't having it. 'It was one random employee's one dumb moment, slipped between quotation marks as though it was policy. I got them to take it out.'

'The FSA's investigation could have quite easily ruined us,' says Barry Gibson, our chairman throughout that difficult period. In hindsight, though, it was probably the best thing that could have happened to the business, and to me, because it made me realise that to treat the customer well, I had to do a lot more than just stick to my own idea of good practice. We went from a business dedicated to selling products to a business dedicated to retaining customers, and that meant refocusing the business's energy on doing the right thing, and while this sounds a bit mealy-mouthed, a bit 'what-he-would-say', I'll stand by it, because I have proof of what we did.

That proof is our success in the US. Naturally the US has regulatory bodies that are there to protect water consumers, and so we had to prove our worth multiple times. What emerged was that, had we not learned from that FSA investigation, we would not have had products and processes that worked and passed regulatory tests in the US. The nightmare we had been through had actually created this massive market opportunity for us. Barry Gibson strongly agrees: 'Our success Stateside would never have happened had we not undergone the FSA investigation, swallowed our medicine and come out changed on the other side.'

To this day, though, Barry frets over how easily we might have spotted this problem had we only been looking in the right direction. 'We should have been alerted by our high repudiation rates. [A repudiation is when a company rejects a claim.] Our rates were high, but, I suppose, using old-school thinking, we saw this as good; we were saving money! But if a product doesn't do what customers expect, they won't renew and will most likely complain.'

Barry's hit here on a key point about our recovery. If we were thinking defensively, then we would want to reject as many claims as possible to improve our margins. Encouraged by our board, though – who were determined we shouldn't paper over any cracks – I and my leadership team turned the problem on its head and we asked ourselves, 'What if we *exceeded* our customers' expectations?'

Our first thought: that'll cost us a fortune. Our second thought: that'll increase our renewal rate. And in a subscription-model business, renewals are where you make all your money. Customer acquisition is costly; customers typically cost us money in the first two years. Profitability comes in year three and beyond, when that customer's satisfaction and loyalty can be considered a steady revenue stream. And so we pivoted, and began to rewrite our policies so as to say 'yes' to the customer, even if it cost us. Barry relishes the irony here: 'All this while, the FSA had been nudging us towards a really good business model! If we embraced it and improved upon it, it would make us much better than anybody else.'

We could have just sat around apologising for our mistakes. Instead, we got in front of them and fostered a different culture. We encouraged our employees to say, 'Yes, we'll sort it out', wherever they could. This generated a tremendous boost in morale: tradespeople were able to flex their skills and help customers and not have to worry about being ticked off or short-changed for their efforts. Imagine you're an engineer. Would you rather go round to somebody's house and say, 'Oh, go on, I can fix that for you.' Or would you sooner go round, suck your teeth and say, 'Well I'll have to ring head office and waste a good hour of my day, and yours, and it'll cost . . .'? Barry has a sister-in-law and likes to think that his being on the board got her to sign up as a HomeServe customer. 'But that wasn't it at all,' recalls Barry. 'It was the fact that the HomeServe bloke who came with his overalls and his bag to fix her leaking bath was such a nice guy and did such a thorough job that it really made her feel very confident and very comfortable.'

If we ignore our small print and say 'yes' to you when you're in a bind, you're very likely to sign up to instant cover, or sing our praises if you're already a customer. Doing you that favour might cost us a few quid, but then, recruiting you in the first place costs us more than a few quid anyway, so who's counting? We're a subscription model, so we'll make a profit eventually. Meanwhile our 'yes' cemented your repeat custom; your repeat custom helps drive down the cost of customer recruitment; and that in turn builds our volumes. It's a virtuous circle.

'Who's counting?' Well, we were, obviously – and to this day the figures bear out our idea. Saying yes is our measurable investment in the customer, and it generates a measurable profit. Did we want to do repairs for people who didn't have a policy? We used to say, 'No, get lost, unless you've got a policy it's tough luck.' Now we said, 'Yes, we'll do it, at a fixed price, a fair rate, and we'll link in a policy for plumbing and drainage (or whatever type of job we have just done) for the next twelve months.' Suddenly we got interest from a whole new group of younger, less insurance-minded customers. We had broadened our market.

'If we hadn't seized the opportunity for change,' says Anna Maughan, 'I honestly think HomeServe would have fallen apart. We're a pretty cohesive bunch, but for a while you could see that while the staff had their pride and the senior management had their good name, there were a few middle managers who said, "I don't want to be associated with this, I'm off." It would have been easy enough to throw blame around, but the feeling was, "You don't turn your back on a friend when they fall on hard times."'

USE WHAT YOU KNOW AGAIN AND AGAIN

Here's a rather less fraught tale of business growth and change. It's about my old friend Simon Blunt, and what he did after he sold the Mortgage Advice Bureau to his successor, Peter Brodnicki, in a management buyout. It's a simple story about pivoting to a new business model. Industry regulation gets a look-in; so does crime.

The story begins in 2004, on one of my 'boys' ski trips'. My friends and I have been terrorising the slopes once a year for about forty years. We're a very mixed bunch skill-wise, mucking in together at a budget hotel so it stays affordable for everybody. Simon remembers: 'Jeremy and I found ourselves queuing up together for a chairlift. We'd got skis on and were shuffling about like penguins – all very awkward – and Jeremy, for something to say, asked me what I was up to. By the time we got off the ski lift, I'd snared him. Not long after, he invested £250,000 in my new idea. Of course, if I had waited ten minutes more, I'd have ended up on the ski lift with you and you would have given me £500,000. But that's life.'

Simon's venture is House Buyer Bureau. It lets you sell a property quickly. A typical house sale can drag on for months, with no guarantee of completion at the end of it. So, the Bureau's a bit like We Buy Any Car: an alternative to auction. If someone wants to sell their house inside of a week, the Bureau can do that. They also buy part-exchange houses on behalf of housebuilders. When people sign 'part exchange' deals, it's not always the housebuilder that's co-signing; it's the Bureau, on their behalf. Simon and Jeremy co-own it now and I lent them a couple of hundred thousand to get going. That's a lot more than the £15,000 Simon lent Jeremy and me in our FastFix days, as I never tire of telling him – and I only charged 10 per cent interest! Then Simon points out to me that my loan was secured on property, whereas his . . . You get the idea. Let's just say we're there for a while.

You'll have seen those advertisements in local newspapers: 'Sell your house for cash!' These property traders had a terrible reputation, and a well-deserved one in many cases. One of their favourite wheezes is to lead you all the way up to exchange of contracts and then drop the price of their offer at the last second. Simon thought, if only an outfit could do this properly, in a more regulated way, everyone would win.

House Buyer Bureau has a sister business, Apex Bridging Loans, which Jeremy is also involved in. Both Apex and House Buyer Bureau are built on accurate property valuation, which makes Apex an excellent example of 'copy and pivot': rather than choosing to do different things every time, Simon repurposed the skill set he'd already mastered to create a new business.

'At the Bureau, we've got to sell everything we buy, so we'd better get the valuation right. Apex, instead of buying properties, lends to small housebuilders. Skill in valuation is crucial here because the development land is our security; it needs to be worth what we think it is.' Simon tells me that bridging-loan companies, which have been around for ever, don't have nearly his company's skill in valuation. They employ chartered surveyors who, quite frankly, aren't going to spend a whole lot of time valuing anything. So now you know why bridging loans are so expensive.

Because Apex values property more accurately than its competition, Simon reckons it can afford to go niche, becoming a sort of 'hands on' bank for the building industry. 'Our bigger competitors will lend you, if you're lucky, 60 per cent of the cost of your project,' he says. 'We've decided to go for a high-profit-margin business. We'll lend 90 per cent. We'll take that chance.'

THE VALUE CHAIN

'How do I help my company grow?' This reminds me of the old Irish joke about the chap who wants to know the way to Dublin. The local savant sucks his teeth and declares, 'Well, I wouldn't start from *here*.'

What kind of company you dream up dictates what level of growth you will attain. I've just been reading about the direct-to-consumer genetics company 23andMe. It'll read your genetic code for you, and even offer you some insights – some sounder than others – about your heritage. The company went public in 2021 with a valuation of $6 billion. By late 2024, its market cap had fallen to around $120 million – a 98 per cent decline. Just now it posted a $667 million loss for its last fiscal year. There are several reasons for its downfall (among journalists, 23andMe has a reputation as the gift that keeps on giving), but the chief one is also the most obvious: customers only ever need to get their genetic code read once. Any future medical breakthroughs that involve mucking about with your genetic code will just read your printout. For 23&Me, that means there's no hope of repeat business. There's no customer relationship. There's no future.

A company designed to spring up like a mushroom after a spring rain, and vanish just as quickly, isn't necessarily a bad idea. But there is a limit to what it can do in the market, and investors will know this. So, the first rule of growing a successful company is, I would say, 'Know who you are.' Are you building a passion project? A pop-up? A bit of a gamble? Or are you in this game for the long haul? If you pretend to yourself that your business is something it's not, you've slit your own throat before you've even begun.

Past a certain point, the rewards you glean from your business will almost entirely be decided by what type of business you are. Ever wondered why there are so many extremely wealthy retailers, but so few manufacturers with the same financial clout? I did – and discovered, when I worked there, that even a giant like Procter & Gamble faced a significant limitation: they didn't control the entire journey of their product from factory to consumer. They manufactured the goods, but then they relied on supermarkets to get those goods into shoppers' hands. Even Procter & Gamble had to negotiate hard for things like prime shelf space and promotional opportunities. Seeing this, I knew I wanted to build businesses that had that final connection with the consumer.

Inside my fridge and bathroom cabinet, you will usually find two of my favourite products. But though I love Gü puddings and King of Shaves, I can't help but feel they could have been even bigger businesses. I first came across them as a judge for the EY Entrepreneur of the Year awards, and despite my enthusiasm, it was obvious they were hamstrung. They didn't own enough of the value chain, and so could never achieve maximum value for their business.

There was, on the other hand, another EY Entrepreneur winner, and his name was Dean Hoyle. Thirteen years after setting it up with a £10,000 loan, Dean sold his greetings card company for £400 million. He achieved such a high value because Card Factory (at least when he ran it) designed, printed and made most of its products in the UK, before selling them direct to consumers in more than one hundred of its own stores. Because Hoyle controlled most of the value chain, his business was worth much more than Gü or King of Shaves.

Billionaires like Simon Arora of B&M, Tom Morris at Home Bargains and Chris Dawson of The Range exert influence over everything except – by and large – the manufacturing process itself. They source direct from overseas factories, design some products, set prices and sell direct to consumers via their own stores. By cutting out the wholesaler, they can offer better prices and still make higher profits.

Exerting this kind of control is known as vertical integration, and it's the key to competitive advantage. In theory, your business becomes more efficient, less costly and more profitable because you own and control supply, production and distribution, from the raw material to the final product. Designing, sourcing, manufacturing, marketing, sales, distribution and aftersales – you are integrating these different capabilities into your business.

There are some businesses that are fully vertically integrated; they even do their own manufacturing. One example is Wren Kitchens, which in 2023 delivered about 130,000 kitchens to homes across the UK. As well as a state-of-the-art factory in Barton-upon-Humber in Lincolnshire, Wren has 111 showrooms in the UK and 13 in the US, each displaying a vast array of kitchens plus the latest virtual-reality design technology, so that people can see their individually designed kitchen before they buy. Wren designs, manufactures, sells, delivers and installs (using approved subcontractors). And because it controls the entire value chain, it keeps its bold environmental promises at every stage.

I'm amazed at how many businesses still only supply to other businesses rather than to consumers as well. Why restrict yourself to being a B2B middleman when B2C is where the real profit is made? Do both, would be my advice: supply and sell. Andrew Nisbet recently sold 80 per cent of his family catering equipment business, Nisbets, for £339 million, and the firm's value is so high because it evolved from pure B2B – supplying hotels, kitchens and canteens – into also selling direct to consumers through twenty-three stores and a hugely popular online offering. Keep your trade customers happy by all means, but have the courage to supply direct to the end consumer as well. Your trade customers won't mind as long as your product or service is good enough. In fact, they might be glad that you're widening your range.

Finally, if you truly want to unlock the growth opportunities in your business, you need to open satellite offices to create opportunities in different regions. Additional Lengths is thinking of opening a salon, training centre and office in central London to gain access to senior talent in the south-east and pick up more customers throughout the south. Checkatrade now has a big new London office for more than two hundred staff, as well as our original office in Portsmouth Harbour where over three hundred colleagues work. A London satellite helps us attract the best talent that doesn't want to work in regions like Yorkshire, my birthplace.

Opening smaller hubs will allow you to access additional London talent in a relatively risk-free and low-cost way. The former UK chancellor, Jeremy Hunt, made this a sight easier for some of us by giving £1 billion in extra funding for new technology hubs around English universities. Instead of relocating, companies looking for tech graduates can now open small offices close to regional campuses, attracting those people without compelling them to settle near a London HQ.

So, there is untapped talent far outside the capital – places where costs are lower and the quality of life is often higher. IWG, the temporary-offices operator, recently published a report showing that large companies, in an effort to get closer to their customers, are setting up smaller offices in commuter towns. This trend is set to increase the number of white-collar workers in those towns 'by 84 to 175 per cent by 2043'.

KEEP YOUR BUSINESS IN SHAPE

Given the radical differences that exist between business types, and even between businesses of the same type, you might seriously doubt that anything useful could be said about business in general. US CEO Tom Rusin seriously doubted that Jim Collins would have much to say to people who (unlike Jim) actually ran businesses. Victoria Lynch taught herself the haircare business at thirteen and has yet to come up for air. Touker Suleyman told me he follows no blueprint, and ascribes his success entirely to fifty years of experience. Craig Waddington's formula for success is even more blunt: work seven days a week for your entire life.

When Steve Hewitt joined Gymshark as CEO, he began to evolve his own ideas about how we think about businesses. He created something called the North Star, a sort of very high-level map – or not even a map, just a figure, a north star, with four points – to help leaders organise their thoughts. The top point, at the pinnacle of the figure, is the purpose of the brand. Why does this brand exist? Why are you going to this much trouble? 'We worked out very quickly that Gymshark was there to unite the fitness community,' Steve says.

Now the two side points. Pointing to the left: the audience. Who do you want to exist for? 'Eighteen- to thirty-five-year-olds were Gymshark's natural demographic, because they constituted what we called "the social net generation": people who lived their lives on social media and were obsessed with fitness.' Most businesses, when they're in their scrappy, entrepreneurial phase, become very opportunistic, but Steve wanted Gymshark to do the exact opposite. 'You can't become a butterfly in the wind, selling to twenty-five-year-old women one week, then deciding to sell to fifty-year-olds the next. Those two demographics shop in completely different places.'

Back to the North Star. And pointing to the right: values. Once you've worked out why you exist and who you exist for, you work out how you're going to behave as an organisation. 'This for me is the crucial point,' says Steve. 'How an organisation behaves is not necessarily how it appears, and in that gap lurk all kinds of hell. If we're one thing to the customer, and another thing entirely to our employees, then the mask will crack very quickly. If our employees aren't enthusiastic about our brand, how are they going to represent us to the customer? So we were very upfront about the kind of people we wanted. If you don't like change – and actually, that's most of us, if we're honest – then Gymshark is not the place for you. We're not an oil tanker. We're still a speedboat, only we're one that – exceptionally among speedboats – manages to travel in a straight line. So if you are used to the corporate world where it's slow, and there's a lot of red tape, and not a lot of risk, then don't say we didn't warn you. Of course, everybody likes the idea of a risky environment. We had a bunch of Nike employees come to us and we, and they, assumed they'd fit right in. But they found themselves having to unlearn stuff they had practised for over twenty years, and we just didn't have the time for them to do that. You can't develop brand values by putting up inspirational posters. You do it by hiring and retaining the right people.'

And at the bottom of Steve's north star? Well, that's the money. 'You don't want some dewy-eyed chief financial officer talking about purpose, audience and values. You want them laser-focused on the business model itself, pulling the levers to accelerate your growth. Why? Because the maths has to work. If the maths doesn't work, you can't live and breathe your purpose. Unless your financial foundations are in place, taking risks and being agile will send you under.

'So that's the North Star. When people ask me, "What got Gymshark from £400,000 to £400 million in sales and unicorn status?", I tell them it was us building the company around those four principles, and being disciplined about it.'

RESILIENCE RULES

'Chance favours the prepared mind.' The French chemist Louis Pasteur is supposed to have said this during his inaugural lecture at the University of Lille in 1854. He meant that sudden flashes of insight and new discoveries don't just happen out of thin air. They occur when someone with the right knowledge and experience is in a position to recognise the significance of something unexpected.

My experience has taught me that chance favours the prepared business. When John Prescott got the water companies to step up for their customers – and by chance nearly destroyed HomeServe's business model – the water companies chose to see a problem, while we went hunting for an opportunity. Were we smarter than the entire UK water industry? Were we braver? Unlikely. But I'm certain we were better prepared. We didn't know what specific rock was coming to knock us off our perch or when, but we had the right culture to survive the knock.

The acid test for us – and for corporate culture in general – came in March 2020, when Covid-19 became a global pandemic. The unfolding crisis was so complex and so immense, it was clear we couldn't afford to wait for perfect knowledge before we took action. I asked Rob Judson, who was then working as global chief operating officer for membership, to lead a task force coordinating responses across the company. This meant transitioning staff to remote work, securing protective equipment and ensuring contractors could safely serve our customers. I lobbied the government to ensure that home emergencies were recognised as critical work, and – putting our money where our mouth was – we offered our repair services for free to frontline NHS staff and care workers. Our technology teams enabled thousands to seamlessly work from home, and we combated the isolation of lockdown however we could. Everything we dreamt up felt like a drop in the ocean, but what else could we do but buckle down?

Our entrepreneurial culture of test-and-release not only saw us through the emergency, it also turned out to be exactly the kind of approach our customers welcomed in those difficult days. Post-lockdown, demand for our home services soared. HomeServe became more resilient than ever – technically, geographically and in its ability to handle future disruptions. The company's focus on people during the crisis cemented trust, leading to record low complaints, increased sales and a strong financial performance. HomeServe's share price reached an all-time high.

I'm not going to sit here and pretend that Covid was good for us; it was horrible for everybody. But there was one aspect of that whole nightmare I do look back on with a smile, and that was the eagerness with which our staff volunteered to come back into the office. That wasn't at all the case in other companies. While a significant proportion of the national workforce were saying they wanted to continue working from home, our people were ringing us up, asking when they could come back to the office. I'm glad we rode the crisis so well, but it's our colleagues' ringing endorsement of our culture that fills me with pride.

LET YOUR BUSINESS ACT ITS AGE

At the end of this road – from starting up to securing investment, to expansion, to maturation – what can your business look forward to? Well, more road would be nice. Companies rise and fall, like any living thing, but a great, mature company can last a very long time, so long as it lives by its values and finds ways to bring those values to bear in an ever-changing marketplace.

Mature companies are not revolutionary. They know already, from experience, what they have to offer the customer. They no longer have to disrupt the market in order to chisel out a place in it for themselves. What they have to do now is embrace the hard graft of constant improvement and adaptation. This is not the sort of work that generates headlines. It's not work that appeals to the more excitable business journalists. It's not even work guaranteed to inspire trust in investors.

Apple found that out when their charismatic leader died. Once Steve Jobs had passed, how was Apple going to remain revolutionary? A lot of the talk among Apple's major investors centred around the gaping hole where they expected Apple's next revolutionary new product to magically appear. Jobs's successor Tim Cook knew – though I doubt he expressed it quite so baldly to the investors – that Apple's revolutionary heyday was over. It had reached that point in its development where it didn't have to disrupt anything, and, indeed, where the only business it could seriously disrupt was its own. What Apple had to do – and what it has continued to do, for well over a decade now – is to constantly refine, improve and adapt its few product lines so that they perfectly fit the needs of the day.

There comes a point where revolutionary products can only eat at each other's market share. Far better to accept when you are on to a winner, and devote your efforts to the continuous improvement of what you do best. The brand proposition of Apple today is simple: they're the only company capable of making a smartphone better than the iPhone 15. It's called the iPhone 16.

Apple was worth $376 billion when Steve Jobs died in 2011. Since then, and for nearly a quarter of a century, the company has released almost nothing new. They've endeavoured to do something much harder: they've made old and trusted things better, again and again and again. They've developed products that lend themselves more to evolution than revolution: services like Apple Pay, Music, Books, TV and iCloud Storage. Today Apple is worth $3.35 *trillion*. That's the power of evolution.

SUMMING UP

Disruption is not a virtue

Talking to young entrepreneurs, I often find them nursing ideas that they imagine are 'disruptive'. I then have to point down the high street and ask them, 'How many truly disruptive businesses do you see out there? How many disruptive businesses do you think the world can handle?'

Then, if my blood is up, I say, 'Think of all those businesspeople who came before you, century upon century of talented and ambitious tradespeople. Do you imagine they opened groceries and bakeries and hardware stores because they couldn't think of anything better to do? Were they "just a bit slow"?'

Businesses exist to serve customers, and customers are our community. We succeed when we make their lives a bit better. We're not here to build monuments to ourselves.

Cash is king

Ensure you generate enough cash to support your growth, maintain returns on capital and weather any unexpected storms. A healthy cash flow is more important than impressive revenue figures.

Adapt and evolve

HomeServe's run-in with the regulator, though a difficult period, forced us to confront our shortcomings, and ultimately led to a stronger, more customer-focused business model. Going the extra mile, though it incurred a short-term cost, won us happier, more loyal customers and a bright future.

Succeed through vertical integration

Controlling as much of the value chain as possible, from sourcing to distribution, can lead to greater efficiency, higher profits and a stronger competitive advantage.

Chapter Eight

Follow a *Not*-to-do List

Last year, when Graham Ruddick invited me onto his business podcast, I found myself quoting Jim Collins, the business guru, and rattling through his brilliant analogy about hedgehogs and foxes. If you're a fox, you're insatiable: you go around snapping up all the ideas you can find and trying them on for size. At the very start of your journey to a billion, you want to be the fox. But soon – much sooner than you think – you've got to become the hedgehog that minds its own business, and knows its own mind, and defends itself fiercely against all comers by putting its prickles up.

As your business expands and the quality of your leadership team rises, you will find yourself sitting in a chair listening, day after day, to lots of good ideas, and you will be saying no to virtually all of them. Be they external consultants, or a focus group, or someone running a customer survey online, or even just someone in the organisation who's had a brainwave, you end up saying 'No' to so many people. It's exhausting, because they almost never come up with *bad* ideas, and you need to maintain the bandwidth to spot the one that might actually work in the business.

Eventually you may discover that the main source of distracting ideas is you. That's the moment you wish you had your replacement lined up, so you could hand over the reins and focus on the part of the business you are best at – or even go and find your satisfaction elsewhere. We start out as buccaneering risk-takers, but in the end we realise that, to succeed, we either need to buckle down or we need to get out of the way. The frustration of being the leader of a mature business is that you can't stray too far from the core without damaging it.

I can think of lots of occasions (I'll run through quite a few of them in this chapter) where I let slip the core of the business to go chasing after shiny things – with predictable results. At such moments I say to myself, 'Clearly, I'm too much of a fox.' But then I'll read something like this, from Anna Maughan: 'One thing that does annoy me about Richard sometimes is that he won't let anything go. He'll say, "Please, find me that paper that we wrote in 2003 about such-and-such." The fact that the world's moved on and the paper's completely irrelevant doesn't faze him in the least. He's constantly thinking, "Oh, we did that once, and maybe if we did *this* to it, it'll work," and so no idea ever dies a decent death. It's like *Groundhog Day*. Who knows what twist Richard is planning, but for us foot soldiers, we're thinking, "Oh God, we're trotting this out again?" But he has to go through the process.'

When you come down to it, we're both foxes and hedgehogs at each and every moment. The fox finds the opportunity, tells the better stories and gets the bigger headlines. The hedgehog generates the wealth. Barry Gibson tells a story about Richard Branson – a hero of my younger years and a notorious fox; his board nicknamed him 'Doctor Yes'. This story neatly reveals both the appeal of foxy behaviour and how, in the long run, it can weaken your position. 'I had the pleasure of working alongside Richard Branson when Virgin Airlines was moving into Heathrow,' says Barry. 'At the time I was managing director of Heathrow Airport and I couldn't help but admire Branson's ability to ignore rules. If he decided that he wanted his plane to arrive at eight o'clock in the morning and he couldn't get a slot through the scheduling system until 11 a.m., his airline would fly the plane over anyway, from New York or Boston. It would arrive with next to no fuel – as is usual for airliners – and of course we had to let it land. What Branson hadn't factored in was the sheer size of Heathrow Airport. It was no trouble at all for us to send his plane trundling down to the other end of the airport to park in a cul-de-sac for a couple of hours until the next free slot opened up. That straightened him out.'

How, as leaders, do we balance fox and hedgehog? We can't go through life telling ourselves not to go chasing after the fun stuff. We'd only make ourselves miserable, and then we'd rebel and do something stupid. We need instead to find positive value in staying disciplined, and sticking to our guns.

One of the best ways to do this, I've found, is to prepare a *not*-to-do list. I mean this literally: get paper and pen and work out all the things that you want to do, and might even be quite good at, but which will take you away from your core business. Make the list long – much longer than your to-do list. Invite contributions. Then, pin the list up above your desk or in your boardroom. Laminate it. Better still, frame it. This is the document that will save you from disaster.

Imagine your business is a vehicle: your purpose is the engine – it propels you. The *not*-to-do list is the steering wheel. It keeps you on your chosen track. It stops you from sliding into the weeds. I'll come back to this idea and explore it a bit more at the very end of this chapter. But let's get some real-world examples under our belt first. I'll show you what happens when fox and hedgehog fall out of balance, and I'll suggest what you can do to stop it from happening.

BEWARE OF SHINY THINGS

Our former chairman Barry Gibson remembers: 'Richard was always very restless and keen to look at adjoining businesses to see if we should move into their territory. And, in all honesty, if you look at all of the businesses that we investigated or bought, very few of them actually succeeded. We learned the hard way that the further they sat from our core, the less likely they were to work.'

While HomeServe was still the Home Service Scheme, and a part of South Staffs, I bought a couple of companies I thought would serve the company's expansion. (The problem with the fox is that it's wily: it talks a good game, and gets you into all kinds of trouble.) I bought Regency, a company that offered extended warranties on things like three-piece suites. The chap who was running it in Weston-super-Mare was doing very well and making quite a lot of money. That convinced me his operation was worth £40 million. Then I bought another business in Norwich that did glazing repairs, locks and so on. This was another little company, very well run and punching above its weight – indeed, turning a £3 million profit. Over the next twelve months, I managed to get it to break even. I don't even remember what I did to Regency, but I promise you it wasn't anything good.

This was around the time my first chairman, Lindsay Bury, was describing me as 'an entrepreneur of genius'. Well, there was a reason for that. We had solved Home Service's business model and were even then turning our money-pit operation into a hugely profitable business. Maybe South Staffs thought I had the golden touch; for sure, they wanted to crow about our success.

Lindsay Bury wrote in his memoir that the board knew that these were bad acquisitions I was making, but they let me go ahead anyway. In retrospect they should have blocked them; I'd have got over it. If I was ever tempted to take Bury's boosterism seriously, our next chairman, Brian Whitty, soon brought me down to earth. It was clear to the entire non-exec team, if not to me, that I had made a couple of really dumb acquisitions, and it was left to Brian to come up with a fitting punishment. He said that, since I'd bought them, I was going to have to go and fix them. Full-time. Commuting between Weston-super-Mare and Norwich. The justice of Brian's punishment made it smart ten times worse. I cavilled. I argued. I may possibly have begged. So far as I remember this was the only time Brian and I ever seriously butted heads.

I didn't go in the end, because I convinced Brian that I would make a complete mess of things. Having invested all this money, we owed it to ourselves to hire somebody who knew how to run those kinds of businesses. For the Norwich company I found Ian Carlisle, who'd been running Autoglass, and he did a fantastic job, bringing the company up to nearly £10 million profit at one point. Still, the businesses did not fit at all well into HomeServe's operation, and there was nothing Ian or anyone could do about that, so in the end we had to let them both go. We sold one to private equity and the other to the management team. I never again made a crucial decision without seeking advice first.

Another big mistake in HomeServe's growth was to expand into too many new products. Along with the furniture warranties and the locks business, there were smart home devices, post-flood and fire restoration work . . . the list of errors goes on and on. These acquisitions weren't totally random. (The fox talks a good game . . .) I had it in mind to turn HomeServe into a one-stop shop dealing with every imaginable domestic emergency. And if we'd called it Every Imaginable Domestic Emergency, I might have seen what an impractical idea it was. Instead, we called it something sensible: the HomeServe Emergency Services Division.

Around 2002, two years before the demerger, we began acquiring businesses that employed their own engineers. This was a significant change as, up to that point, we had relied entirely on subcontractors. Highway Emergency Services Ltd was our first such acquisition. After the demerger we bought Chem-Dry, a franchise business specialising in fire and flood restoration. Then we bought Sergon, which ran a network of independent contractors carrying out plastering, decorating and building repairs on damaged properties.

To attract sufficient trade, we pivoted away from the consumer (not all pivots are sensible) towards providing emergency repair services to household insurers – a B2B model, in other words, and an unconscious return to our very earliest business, Professional Properties. On paper, HomeServe Emergency Services Division had it all, offering insurers every imaginable claim repair service: fire and flood restoration, glazing, locks, window and door frames, drainage repairs, permanent building repairs . . . But it was a B2B business, and what happens to B2B businesses? Sooner or later, they get screwed.

Our new MD, Jonathan King, could see this coming a mile off. I didn't want to be grumpy with him, but I had to say something: 'You know, you're the only one who doesn't support this!' I should have listened. It's easier to make money from many small customers than from a few large customers. In the core HomeServe business, we had many small customers who bought directly from us. They put a value on peace of mind and so they weren't particularly price-sensitive. I don't mean they had money to burn – I mean that, once we set our price, we knew our customers wouldn't then try to haggle for a lower one.

HomeServe Emergency Services' customers, meanwhile, were big insurance companies, or rather, their procurement departments, whose job it is 'to screw you down on price every year' (to quote Jonathan). 'It's not difficult for them to find someone who'll do the job cheaper. Either you reduce your price and margin or you lose the business. This was around the time electronic reverse auctions were coming in. You could sit there in front of a screen – I did this – and watch your margins being chopped to pieces by bids so low, you knew you were in a race to the bottom.'

Another mistake we made was to buy small, owner-operated businesses that already had relationships with the insurance companies. We'd impose controls and systems, increasing our costs and theirs, all to fix a machine that had been working perfectly well before we turned up. Our hoped-for profits did not appear. In 2009, we announced that we were selling off Highway, Sergon, Improveline and Chem-Dry at a loss of £97 million. Altogether we spent £130 million of borrowed money and HomeServe profit, only to write off the best part of £100 million. There was one small ray of sunshine: the market rewarded us for focusing again on our fantastic core membership business. On the day we wrote off £100 million, our share price went up and increased the value of HomeServe by £250 million!

It's easy to be nimble when you're small. If a small company gets something wrong, people just chalk it up to its learning process. The larger your company gets, though, the more numerous its responsibilities. When a big company makes a mistake, people immediately assume a lack of judgement. For the leadership, it gets safer to say 'No' to an idea than to back a new venture into unknown territory.

By the summer of 2012, I felt this was happening to us (the fox talks a good game . . .) and we created our very own 'shed' – a small, independent team that would focus on developing innovative projects. Led by Greg Jackson (as it happens, another graduate of Procter & Gamble's marketing department, and later the founder-CEO of Octopus Energy), in the course of three years the Shed evolved into HomeServe Alliance, a division out to corner the market in new boiler installations in the UK.

That business lasted only three years – but this time, this was what we had expected and had planned for. This time we weren't trying to conquer the universe; we were trying to kick-start a new innovation culture at HomeServe. By limiting our expectations and establishing a clear purpose for our experiments, we sowed the seeds for HomeServe's future – in particular, our evolution into heating installations. The fox can be your friend, so long as you leash it.

I asked Barry Gibson about the HomeServe Shed, expecting a comfortable conversation about how well we had corralled and directed our entrepreneurial spirit. Barry is the man who once said, 'It's perfectly reasonable for a company of our size to be investing five to ten million pounds a year in research and development, because out of that may come a business that one day will be worth one billion pounds.' What I got was a lot of ribbing. 'Richard, of course, will say that there is no such thing as an unworkable good idea – that everything can be tweaked and pivoted into submission. And maybe he's right. He's proved his point a few times. But entrepreneurs have a tendency only to see the upside of a venture. For example, Servowarm. Why on earth did we buy Servowarm? It was a third-rate boiler installer who decided at some point it wanted to package service agreements up with its products. And, on the basis of that, and only that, we bought a third-rate company at a first-rate price and crashed it.

'That was not our only loss-making exit. There are quite a few businesses that we looked at and got excited about only to discover, when we got hold of them, that they weren't the kinds of businesses we had expected at all. You thought you were buying an orange and ended up with a lemon. Of them all, the only ones that did well were the local heating installation businesses we acquired.'

WHEN TO LET GO OF GOOD IDEAS

Most of the stories I've told so far in this chapter have been about the fox getting out of control. They're war stories, and amusing, but we should dig deeper. Here's a story about a business idea that we all agreed was very much part of our core. It took a lot of time, and a lot of money, for us to discover otherwise.

The lesson of the fox and the hedgehog is an important one, but it's not always obvious where the hedgehog stops and the fox begins. You will make mistakes, and then your survival will depend on how good your Plan B was, or even your Plan C. The project I have in mind was called Leakbot – an innovative idea that emerged organically from the work we were doing in our Shed. The idea sprang from an observation that insurance companies suffer their biggest losses through leaking pipes. What happens in domestic situations is that a pipe develops a leak, and eventually either the pipe bursts or the amount of water leaking from the pipe over time causes so much damage it leads to some other critical failure – typically a ceiling falling in.

Leakbot appeared while we were dabbling in the disaster recovery business, hoping this would be a good way to sell people on the idea of becoming HomeServe members. In our plans, we had the idea to develop new products. We came across a professor who was trying to build something around the fact that the temperature of the water coming from the mains through your domestic supply pipe is a sight colder than the ambient temperature of your house. If the pipe gets colder, it tells you water is running into the property. Now, if you put a device on the supply pipe that can detect a temperature change in the pipe, and it detects this at an unlikely hour of the day – 3 a.m., say – then (and especially if the flow was constant), you can be pretty certain that there's some uncontrolled flow that needs investigating.

Greg Jackson took this idea and ran with it, and the result was Leakbot, a device so simple and straightforward the consumer could fit it without fuss to their own supply pipe. If it detected a leak, it would alert the insurer, who would then press a button to get a HomeServe engineer to go round and fix the leak for around £50.

That's no small saving, given the alternative: say, a ruined living room and an insurance claim for £5,000. The technology was hard to perfect, but it worked well in the end.

It was at that point that we hit a wall: insurers were reluctant to call up their customers and tell them they needed a device fitted to their pipework. They just didn't have that level of trust with their customers. No one did when it came to that sort of technology – witness, a short while later, the painfully slow roll-out across the UK of smart meters for gas and electricity. Here we were with a product that could save our sister industry untold amounts of money, and though several insurers took up the idea – I think Hiscox marketed it to their high-net-worth customers as an exclusive perk – the results were disappointing.

Leakbot was a good idea, very well executed. But good ideas cost a lot of money, and you can get frighteningly far down the road before evidence emerges that your good idea is not going to set the market alight without a lot of painstaking preparation.

Leakbot thrives under new ownership, and HomeServe still has a shareholding. Craig Foster, who led the Leakbot team, has built a successful business around it called Ondo InsurTech, which is now a separate listed company, free to bring in other investors, explore new opportunities and grow as a standalone business.

What's the lesson here? Perhaps it's that not every good idea is going to turn out good for *you*. In those circumstances, you have to swallow your pride and roll with the punches. Leakbot is much better off in an agile setting of its own.

THE LEADERSHIP TRAP

'There are three things you need to run a business,' Jonathan King said to a researcher of mine, 'and Richard is good at two of them. The first is having a high-level vision. The second is attention to detail. I've seen Richard have a big idea and launch straight into writing the marketing pack, down to the application form. But he's hopeless at the stuff in the middle – the drudgery of making it happen.'

How do people handle a leader who's too much of a fox? 'Richard is the sort of leader who will wander into the office, talk to a marketing manager and give them five ideas. People whose job it is to manage the managers often hate that sort of thing, but I never minded. The challenge was to explain to my staff, "Look, just because these ideas are coming from Richard doesn't make them tablets carried down from the mountain."

'Richard's risky because he's smart and he doesn't have a filter. A lot of his ideas are good, but they're mixed in with a good amount of garbage. Richard describes how he wants the world to be, and that gives him a kind of aura. Your job is to make things conform to that vision, and ideas about how to get there could come from anywhere, including from the most junior member of your team. It's your job to decide, without fear or favour, which ideas will get you to where you want to go.'

Any direct report with a strong entrepreneurial leader who has effective control finds it very hard to say to them, 'No, you can't do that,' for fear of not getting invited back to the party. So, leaders actually have to encourage those dissenting voices and listen to what they say. It's an important skill that entrepreneurs don't learn easily.

Anna Maughan remembers, 'When we first started the HomeServe business, the culture of HomeServe was a bit "Richard told me to do this, so I've got to rush off and do it straight away". Well, a start-up is a start-up. But you really need to move away from that kind of thinking the moment you start to grow. If the leader tells you to do something, and you think there's something not quite right, you've got to be able to stop them in mid-flow and bring up that worry. If something goes wrong, you've got to be able to go up to them and say, "We're in trouble."'

The larger your organisation, the more levels it has, the more people will think politically and police their speech. I wonder if there's a critical number, a certain size your business has to get to, before signals start getting muffled? The psychologist Robin Dunbar has noticed that people, left to their own devices, will gather in groups that rarely number above 150. The number comes up in all kinds of places. During the Second World War, a company (the smallest military unit that can stand alone) consisted of around 170 men. A mid-1990s study commissioned by the Church of England concluded that the ideal size for congregations was 200 or fewer – large enough to support the activities of a church, small enough for everyone to know everyone else well enough to form a close-knit, supportive community. Then there are the Hutterites, Christian pastoralists whose communes rarely expand above 100 people. When they get to 150 members, they split. The Hutterites say that once a community exceeds 150 people, it becomes increasingly difficult to control. It's no longer enough, if someone is misbehaving, to go and have a quiet word with them in a corner of the field.

Your job as leader is to create a company that minimises the downside that comes from exceeding (often hugely exceeding) the Dunbar number. One way, much discussed, is to keep your organisation as 'flat' as possible, so there aren't too many gatekeepers between the emperor and the boy who sees he's not wearing any clothes. 'We built a £400 million business in an environment where the leadership team was always super-accessible,' says Steve Hewitt, reflecting on his time at Gymshark. 'I didn't have an office. I sat out with the troops. My office-mood barometer was whoever was organising the line for the restaurant. They could tell me what the vibe was that day far better than HR could.'

It occurs to me as I write this that what Steve was building here was (fun fact) the exact opposite of what Louis XIV built around himself at the Palace of Versailles. You see, for his own survival, the seventeenth-century French king had to make sure that his aristocracy were completely hamstrung, powerless and incapable of coherent action. So, he built himself a sort of anti-business in Versailles, bestowing titles – around two hundred different grades of nobility and patronage, each with its own duties and privileges – on a court that never topped a thousand people. The courtiers were so busy jostling with each other they forgot to topple the king. That was then. This is now. Don't be Louis. Be Steve. Be me:

whenever I walked through one of our call centres the room would erupt with requests (some genuine, some sarcastic) for free helicopter rides.

UGLY TRUTHS AND HOW TO HEAR THEM

Sorting out your organisation's structure is certainly important, but I would also reiterate what Jonathan said earlier: culture beats process every time. As leader, you carry the major responsibility for setting the tone for your business. This requires courage and integrity (more about these and other entrepreneurial qualities in the next chapter) but also vigilance.

'I don't think we've yet reached the size where people routinely, even subconsciously, shield me from ugly truths,' says Ben Francis of Gymshark (two thousand employees as I write this; about four hundred in its head office). 'But I can see it's a problem waiting in the wings. With new senior hires, I've noticed there's a short period in which we're sussing each other out, and then they're coming in with problems as they occur because, frankly, none of them are going to be their fault. After that, a certain guardedness sets in, which it's up to me to break down. You want a relationship strong enough to withstand difficult conversations. The stronger the relationship, the easier the conversations go. Our head of brand is a joy: "Well, Ben," he says, bursting into the office, "I royally f – – – d that up." With the others, I have to push a little more.'

As you get more senior, people find it harder to have those sorts of brutal conversations with you, and you have to work harder to convince people: 'Look, do me a favour and just tell me the facts!' I reckon all leaders need someone like my oldest son, Tom. He completely missed the lesson on how to sugar a pill. 'I think you can do much better on your social media,' he said to me the other day. 'And the quality of your video production is nowhere near good enough.'

'Ah!' I said. 'Right you are.'

'You can also improve your content.'

'Right,' I said.

'You need to.'

'Okay,' I said.

You need to improve it, Dad . . .'

I gritted my teeth and booked myself some urgent media training.

I need to listen when people say to me, these are the things that are not going well, and these are the things you're not good at. That is really important. I don't find it hard to admit that I still make lots of mistakes and I still need help to get better. It's an essential part of my job.

FIND YOUR RED THREAD

It's easy to discipline a leader. In my experience, you just hold out the prospect of a full-time job in Norwich. (Sorry, Norwich.) But how do you discipline a company? How do you make out a *not*-to-do list for hundreds, thousands, tens of thousands of people? You can't just stand there telling people not to do things. (They really will mutiny.) You need some guard rails, though, otherwise you've got chaos.

You need forums that encourage and channel your business's creative energy back into your business. Shopify came up with a great idea early on: once a quarter, the company holds Hack Days, during which individuals or teams develop an idea that the business can invest in and build. In the days leading up to Hack Day, people are conversing across departments to develop unusual ideas. At the end of the day there are presentations and prizes. The prizes are just a bit of fun, but the ideas are dead serious, and if they're carried forward, then the winners share in the profits their idea has generated.

Something else you can do – and this takes us right back to the beginning of this book – is tell the company story so well, your own people will tell it, verbatim, to each other and to your customers. Here's Gymshark's Ben Francis: 'I love Land Rover. The first Land Rover, built in 1948, was the best off-roader ever made. Today, the best off-roaders are still Land Rovers. They've maintained that red thread of excellence and authenticity, and it's widened their appeal to the point where – and who saw this one coming? – you can hardly move in London for all the parents driving their little darlings to school in Range Rovers.' Land Rover doesn't and never has marketed its vehicles for the school run. It markets to its reputation as the creator of the Defender. It's diversified to a degree, but it's never let go of that red thread – and doing that, being that disciplined, has *increased* its popularity. 'Well, Gymshark's like Land Rover,' says Ben. 'We do gym. We're a bunch of gym obsessives. Why, really, would you want to come and work for us if you *weren't* a gym obsessive? Gym is all we do! We want to build a hundred-year brand, so it's not good for us to be okay at lots of things. We have to be really good at one thing. We have to be narrow on brand and product. We don't do "athleisure" or sports casual. The gym is our red thread. Some people love Gymshark because it speaks to them. Others will never buy it because it's too gym-focused.'

Now that, I hardly need point out, leaves a huge market in the middle that up to now Gymshark has not addressed: people who don't go to the gym much but are intrigued by the story the brand is telling. And since Gymshark's leaders want to grow the company, they're going to have to find a way to diversify without diluting. 'So what we're trying to do is to use bricks-and-mortar stores to sell the "just do gym" message to a larger audience,' Ben comments. 'While everyone else in the sports and fitness sector seems to be going broad and watering themselves down, we want to do a Land Rover and have people buy what we make because it's special and out of the ordinary.'

Like all great ideas, this one has a precedent. Lots of people wear Barbour's famous waxed jackets – far more than live and work in the countryside. Walk into one of Barbour's stores, though, and you'll find they've stayed true to their core: their range is impressive, but there's nothing there that doesn't belong in the countryside. Upstairs, just to complicate matters, you'll find Barbour International, which looks very different. But dip into the history and you'll see how this odd coupling came about, and why it works.

Barbour International was spun out in 1936 to 'do a Barbour' with motorcycle clothing, and while the two brands share bricks and mortar, they've always kept strictly apart; if anything, they've emphasised their differences.

Barbour is selling you the idea of the countryside, Barbour International is selling you the idea of motorcycling. And now Gymshark is selling you the idea of gym. Three successful brands: each with a unique story to tell.

The discipline you need to hold the business together comes not from centralising functions or barking at people; it comes from telling a story engaging enough that your people want to spread it. Who doesn't want to be part of a good story?

Brand stories are just one more way to focus your team's creativity on the needs of the business. Hack days and the like offer a more structured path to the same goal. I think both depend for their success on the leader's commitment. Authenticity is key. There's nothing more likely to inspire contempt among your people than some outsourced bonding activity that pretends everyone's part of some big happy family. We've all seen *Squid Game*. We don't need it at work.

We need leaders who can look past their own private enthusiasms and show commitment to their business's core idea. We need them to tell their brand story, and we need to see them choke up at the thought of it. We need to see their passion.

Your *not*-to-do list is not there to reduce your happiness. It's there to help you discover what makes you most happy. For the business, it's not about squashing people's enjoyment. It's about finding joy in a common goal.

SUMMING UP

Three little questions

One of my greatest strengths is also a weakness – I'm always looking to grab a fresh opportunity, sometimes to the detriment of what I already have. But by resolving to do less, I've become better at the things that matter most.

Sometimes the hardest thing in business is to say 'No'. Our natural instinct is always to want to do more. We're too often seduced by the prospect of spending money on acquiring something, which often fails to get the promised-for shareholder return, instead of disposing of an asset that underperforms or no longer fits.

We need to realise that the less we choose to do, the more we will achieve. A well-lived life demands that we focus our time and energy on what truly matters. Saying 'No' to non-essential requests and opportunities frees us up to make our highest contributions. And, once we've determined our priorities, safeguarding our time and energy ensures that those things get done with excellence. Far better to do one or two things really well.

To keep us focused, as we contemplate yet another 'golden opportunity', here are three questions we should ask ourselves:

1. What am I passionate about?
2. At what can my business be the best in the world?
3. What drives my business's economic engine?

Write the answers in one sentence and that will be your guide to what you do and – just as important – what you shouldn't do.

Develop your focus

Focus on doing one or two things exceptionally well. Deliberately choosing not to pursue certain opportunities gives you the time and resources to excel at your core.

Know when to say 'No'

Regularly evaluate products or ventures that no longer serve your strategy or are dragging down your performance. Don't hesitate to let those things go. Create a conscious list of things to avoid. This provides needed clarity and keeps you from getting derailed.

Beware of shiny objects

Be vigilant about acquisitions or expansions that don't truly align with the heart of your business. When it comes to technology, beware of hype. Ask yourself: how will new technologies (like AI) improve what you already do well? Don't get distracted by the next big thing for its own sake.

Chapter Nine

Hone Your Character

Half of all entrepreneurs are born. The entrepreneurial bug is lodged in their genes. The other half fall into entrepreneurial business in later life. In both cases, there are certain personal qualities common to entrepreneurs, and if you have none of these qualities, you'd be better off finding a different vocation. Still, you'd be a pretty unfortunate person not to have at least a few of the qualities entrepreneurialism requires.

I certainly don't display easily all the qualities I'm going to explore in this chapter. But I've learned, first of all, to play to my strengths. I've worked on what I know I'm good at, and I've become *very* good at it. I've also learned what I'm missing, and how to spot those qualities in others. Those were the people I needed to have by my side if I was ever to achieve success.

COURAGE

There are umpteen kinds of courage, of course. Was it courageous of me to go to my board and say, 'I want to buy this business called Checkatrade for £74 million'? I think so: at the time, Checkatrade was making only a million pounds of profit.

There is a kind of courage – the courage to get your own way – that tips easily into foolhardiness. A surer kind of courage comes from honesty. It's not easy to be the bearer of bad news, and even harder if you're the cause of it. It's not easy to disagree fundamentally with someone and say so. It's not easy to put honesty before convenience. But, though it may take a while, it's a winning move, every time. (We'll return to this idea in a second, when we consider the value of integrity.)

The best kind of courage comes when we accept our own limitations. There are things we don't know and things we can't do, so let's admit the fact. This is the kind of courage we feel even if we're feeling afraid, even if we're feeling inadequate. It's the courage of an open mind, and it prompts us to push ourselves beyond our comfort zone.

Leaders must show courage, even when courage itself has deserted them. That effort, if it goes awry, can corrupt a person. One moment you're projecting your best self to comfort others, the next you're telling yourself you're better than you really are. Braggarts are made that way, and braggarts become bullies.

Where can you find the courage to lead, even when courage has deserted you? You'll find that courage in recognising and admitting your own limitations, and then, without even thinking about it, doing something about them. You'll find it by listening to people. It's never a sign of weakness to change course because of advice or negative results. If you're willing and able to pivot when facing new realities, you're someone the business needs. There are plenty of disasters – Kodak, Nokia, Yellow Pages – where leadership was so very confident no one felt able to make the challenge necessary to rapidly evolve those business models away from disaster.

Of course, for the plan to go wrong in the first place, you do actually have to have a plan. A concrete plan. If you're the kind of leader who walks into a meeting asking, 'So what do you all think we should do?', I don't hold out much hope for you. What's more frightening than a plan that goes wrong? A plan that makes you look silly. Well, buckle up, because the *very worst* thing you can do, in business as in life, is to be too afraid to ask the daft question, or stifle an idea because it may make you look a bit daft. Like this one, maybe: 'I have twelve rabbits, Flopsy, Mopsy, Topsy . . . Flopsy is worth 2p, Mopsy is worth 4p, Topsy has just had 12 babies, each of which can be sold for 1p . . .'

Surround yourself with people who feel able to challenge you, and thicken your skin so you're ready to be challenged. Don't stack the deck with those who think like you or have the same backgrounds. Very often, the best advice comes from people who see things differently because they've had different experiences. 'Diversity' has become, I know, a buzzword bandied about by people who seem to want us all to think alike. But don't let's abandon the original idea. The great joy of today's trend for reverse mentorship is finding wisdom from younger generations and junior managers with experiences that – in a world that turns on a penny – are quite as valuable as our own.

Finally, let's all make an effort to recognise the courage in others. For instance, I've met male investors who think female entrepreneurs are more averse to risk-taking. That's nonsense. It's true that women tend to be more sensitive to financial losses than men, but that doesn't mean they won't take risks. It means their approach to risk is more considered and sensible. And if overcoming obstacles is an index of courage, then women's courage is a source we can ill afford to ignore. A recent report suggested that if women entrepreneurs received the backing to start and scale at the same rate as men, the UK would benefit from an extra £250 billion worth of growth. But they don't. The Alison Rose Review of Female Entrepreneurship found that only 5 per cent of venture capital money goes to female entrepreneurs.[*]

Of my Growth Partner investments, 40 per cent have female founders – a higher ratio when compared to most private equity players. I don't subscribe to gender targets. When you chase numbers, mediocrity results. It's not that mediocre people get promoted. It's that businesses respond in half-hearted ways, ticking boxes rather than truly investing in female talent. They are chasing numbers rather than doing the hard work of building a robust culture where women feel valued and supported.

One of the most significant decisions I took at HomeServe was to fast-track female talent. Motherhood and family care shouldn't affect career trajectories, so our Summit Programme enabled female managers to jump a level in qualification criteria when they took time

---

[*] HM Treasury (2019) 'The Alison Rose Review of Female Entrepreneurship', 8 March. Available online at www.gov.uk/government/publications/the-alison-rose-review-of-female-entrepreneurship.

out to start a family or care for loved ones. It's been great to see one of those who benefited from the scheme in the US, Deb Dulsky, thrive as chief executive of the building services firm SafeBasements. The more we divide men and women, the more we strengthen the status quo. We need to work together.

CURIOSITY

For all the sacrifices my parents made to send me to a good school, I didn't do very well there. I was more interested in business. And I only got to study economics at York by camping outside the admissions officer's door. I knew what I wanted from my education, and I absorbed it all. But I didn't walk away thinking I knew very much. Rather, I felt I had been given a much clearer idea of what I didn't know.

And so, to this day, I read, constantly, voraciously, snapping up not just the war stories of other business leaders (entertaining as they are) but academic analyses, psychology, history – whatever I think will enrich my life and my business. We're only here once, so why ever would we want to stop learning about the world around us? And with the books comes a daily diet of business news and case studies – especially those from *Business Leader* and Growth Partner. Sometimes Ryan, my management assistant, will put together a brief on a company that someone's mentioned, and we'll spend some time analysing it and figuring out how the business model works. Of course, I listen to a lot of books, too – even in the eight minutes it takes me to run from my front door in Marylebone to the gym and back (at 1.4x speed so I can get through them quicker).

My kids tease me about how many books I cram into my cabin bag for the summer holiday, but my worst fear is running out of them. They bought me a Kindle for Christmas so I can be more efficient with my packing and less anxious about running out of books.

There are many ways of learning about the world in addition to books. I have huge admiration and respect for people who just want to get on with life and learn by doing. In 2001, I invested £1 million to ensure that one in five of HomeServe's workforce were apprentices. Learning is the only way people can get further in life, and if I'm looking for a first hire, it's far more important to me as an employer to know how fast and how well you can learn. When you start out, what you already know is not much more to me than a 'nice-to-have'.

For years, UK governments have pumped money into sending people to universities that can barely afford to maintain decent libraries, and this catch-all keep-'em-quiet-for-another-three-years attitude has robbed us of a generation of artisans, specialists and craftspeople. Why are we cramming academic knowledge down young people's throats when there are so many other kinds of knowledge out there?

Between thinking you know what's happening because you read performance indicators and satisfaction ratings, and actual experience, there is very often a chasm. It's why we give new recruits at HomeServe the chance to spend a day accompanying an engineer in their van, learning from the ground up.

The chief executive of Marks & Spencer, Stuart Machin, recently revealed that to pass their annual review, all his 3,800 staff (including those that are normally office based) will have to spend seven days a year on the shop floor – 'proper work', as he calls it. (Stuart, who started as a teenage shelf-stacker at his local supermarket, has transformed that company, doubling the share price and returning it to the FTSE 100 after a four-year absence.)

I dedicate a significant chunk of my time – probably 20 per cent of my working week – to networking, meeting people and learning from their experiences. Curiosity is one of the essential traits of leadership and – take it from this bookworm – you can't get it all from books. When the business comes alive in front of you, full of all the details that you'd never see from behind a desk, you will uncover insights no presentation can ever match.

INTEGRITY

Integrity is not the same as honesty (I hope we can take honesty for granted). Integrity is about living and behaving in a way that embodies your values. I remember, during the mis-selling crisis of 2011 (see Chapter Seven), I was spending twelve hours a day in back-to-back meetings and the rest of the day frantically trying to prepare for the day after. Everyone was asking me whether HomeServe was going to go bust. We were dealing with problem after problem and the share price was crashing. Throughout, I had to embody the values of the company. I had to project an image of strength and honesty, transparency and confidence.

Did I feel, just then, as though I was the paragon of all those virtues? Not so much. But I had to help maintain the integrity of the company by acting sure and strong. Integrity is not about revealing your authentic self. It's about acting up to your best idea of yourself, for everyone's sake, and even if, in that moment, that best self seems a remote memory.

Leaders have to worry about their own integrity (of course), and also about the integrity of their business (how an organisation behaves is not necessarily how it appears). But it's a different kind of integrity I want to talk about here. How do leaders communicate with integrity through what may be a complex, many-layered organisation?

This is, traditionally, the job of a chief of staff, and up until recently I've drawn people for this role from the world of commerce, but when I was last hiring for a chief of staff, I went and got myself someone with over a decade's experience of government. Hannah Guerin was senior special adviser to the then UK Home Secretary Priti Patel. Her background is predominantly in Number 10, sorting out Prime Minister's Questions, and in the Home Office. In those environments, you don't have time to mess about; every minute counts. She's used to being attached to the news cycle, where things need to be done very quickly. And because she's from government, she looks at problems from different angles that aren't all about money.

This matters because entrepreneurs think about money all the time. It's not that we're greedy (or not necessarily). Money just happens to be the fluid through which we move. We think about money the way lumberjacks think about trees, or fishermen think about fish. Is this entirely healthy for us? No, not entirely. And it's refreshing to be working with someone who doesn't know everything there is to know about money, but can see immediately what our work represents and what effects we're having in the wider world.

Being in government has taught Hannah how to negotiate, how to find the right people, how to have the confidence to get stuff done, how to push things forward, how to deliver and, in particular, how to deliver at pace. She's given me a whole new appreciation of the news cycle, and how, in a digital age, things can go wrong very quickly and reputational damage can be severe.

Her *not*-to-do list is longer than mine. She says that's because, in government, you get really pushed around. 'You have a set timeline in which to deliver. You're either in or you're out. You've got a set parliamentary timetable to legislate. You've got a certain window where the opportunity might be there, or it might not be. You're constantly recalibrating, particularly in the Home Office, to survive each day, based on what's going to trip you up politically versus what policy will actually deliver the most benefit for people. So the *"not*-to-do" list is important. The pet projects have to go on there for another day unless you've got a different way to deliver them, because you can become busy very quickly.'

Hannah's role is both to deliver the ugly truth to me when no one else feels able to say it, and to represent me, on a weekly basis or even more often, to people who – time pressures being what they are – may not see me in person from one quarter to the next. And this is where the business of integrity comes in: part of Hannah's role is to take meetings for me, to speak on my behalf and to articulate what I would say if I were there. 'To do that, you have to really understand the person and be confident in the views you're expressing,' she says. 'You can't overstep the mark. It can be quite dangerous; if it seems to people that you don't have that relationship and know-how, then people won't trust you, and the organisation won't follow.' Sometimes I'll say something without really understanding how it's going to be executed. Then Hannah has to translate my intent, and break down and discuss the challenges of making it happen.

I mentioned earlier the idea that organisations should be kept as 'flat' as possible. One of the reasons this is so helpful is because people with Hannah's skill set are in such short supply. 'The more layers there are in an organisation, the more the truth can be diluted,' says Hannah. 'Few people, deep down, believe that their organisation is truly one team.'

LOW EGO

One of the perks of creating a business is that you get to meet incredible business leaders in person. Most of them are remarkably humble – even shy. They look at the people around them, judge their abilities and their actions, and conclude that they should probably downplay their own involvement. They understand that they're not excellent at everything, they can't even *do* everything, and so they surround themselves with people who are better than them.

A lot of people shy away from employing people who are smarter than them. They feel threatened, or they think the board will notice and make them redundant, or they simply imagine they'll be so overwhelmed that they'll lose their identity and purpose. As someone who makes a point of employing people smarter than I am, let me assure you: none of that happens. All that happens is that your organisation improves. So, you can apply for a job and be a good cultural fit and a stand-up colleague, but if you're not brighter than me, then I'm losing out, and I'm going to carry on looking.

Am I humble? Not in the sense that I think it's the best way of interacting with other people. For me, low ego is a necessary mindset if I'm going to consume as much information from people as possible. Unless I show a certain level of humility, no one's ever going to want to satisfy my curiosity, and – a key point – unless I controlled my ego, I probably wouldn't be listening properly anyway.

'Ego is a business-killer,' says Steve Hewitt. 'The number of people I've met who think they're the smartest in the world is unbelievable. Couple that attitude with a bit of success and – well, we know the sort of people I'm talking about. You mention your holiday in Tenerife and the next thing you know they're showing you their snaps of Elevenerife. If a new hire couldn't build the right environment, based on the values that we had at Gymshark, then we either didn't employ them or we exited them very quickly. There's no point doing anything else.'

The difficulty with low ego is in how you express it, or whether you can even express it at all. In the UK we downplay our achievements on the assumption that the listener is reading between the lines. You know the sort of thing: you storm the beachhead and your commander asks how the operation went and you report, 'Not too shoddy, sir!' Or Jonathan King arrives back at HomeServe in the middle of the mis-selling crisis and sees that we're in 'a bit of a state'.

This sort of thing doesn't work quite so well in America – and there I go with the British understatement again! Let me try that again. Understatement and the show of humility are disastrous tactics in a US business meeting. I've been kicked under the table by my team many times for listing all my many mistakes and failures. Americans only want to hear about your successes. But here's the odd thing: the American business environment is much more forgiving of failure than we are in the UK. As you'd expect, many American entrepreneurs have had many failed businesses before they achieved their success. No one in the US imagines that you can escape this trial-by-fire. And yet, no one who comes out the other side and survives ever shares their war stories – not in a face-to-face meeting, anyway. There's a sort of unspoken agreement never to mention the elephant in the room. For a poor Brit, it's very confusing.

NON-CONFORMITY

When I started to think about the entrepreneurial personality, 'non-conformity' was the first characteristic I wrote down. And yet it's the one that's proving the hardest to write about. I think what's tripping me up is that 'non-conformist' conjures up an image of a person who is messy, ornery and difficult: someone who, by poking sticks at it, demonstrates their infatuation with the establishment. None of the entrepreneurs I know have nearly enough time in the day for games of that sort.

Do I mean that entrepreneurs are eccentrics? After all, eccentrics are often monomaniacally obsessed with something. But the uselessness of that 'something' is pretty much the point: brilliant cartoon inventions like W. Heath Robinson's 'Multimovement Tabby Silencer' and Rube Goldberg's 'Automatic Back Scratcher' (involving a napkin, a spoon, a parrot and a rocket) come to mind. Entrepreneurs are famous for 'thinking outside the box', but they do so to some purpose, you would hope.

Also, entrepreneurialism has more to do with picking the locks on difficult problems than declaring war on business-as-usual (so called because it usually makes money). So 'contrarian' and 'radical' are out.

In exasperation, I turn to an old notebook and I find this:

5 a.m.	Wake up. Gym kit on. Breakfast. Jump into car. (There's a driver, so I'm free to answer emails.)
7.30 a.m.	Outdoor swim, rain or shine. (I'm going to be wet anyway, what does it matter?) Gym. Put on suit.
8.30 a.m.	Back in the car for phone calls.
9 a.m.	Arrive at the office. Time to begin the day!

At HomeServe, this used to be my morning routine. It still is, but for a few details. (Less commuting time. A short run from my house in Marylebone to the gym. A covered pool.) Journalists used to make a thing of my boundless energy. The *Mail on Sunday* had me down as 'the emergency man in a hurry', who 'leaps out of helicopters on skis and can't wait to turn HomeServe into a global giant'. The journalist also said that, at forty-four, I came across like a 'desperately eager twenty-five-year-old'. No one who's met me is going to quibble with that.

And this sets me thinking about my mother Philippa, a very energetic woman. Her secretary, who was about twenty-five years younger than her, once complained, 'It's all right for you, you don't get tired...'

Is all this energy of mine inherited? Should I do a 23&Me and start marketing the Harpin Chromosome™? On the other hand, if I'm such a superman, why am I such a reluctant runner? (I'll do it – just don't ask me to enjoy it.) Why, after forty-odd years, has my aggressive determination to ski left me with such terrible style and technique? And why, if I'm so naturally fit and healthy, am I unable to muster the most meagre defence against the second Gü pudding?

The more I think about it, the more ordinary I seem to myself – and thank goodness for that, because, if that's the case, then I can only be getting my energy from the same place everyone else gets theirs: from enjoying what I do. I love my life and, for me, nothing is more precious than time. These days I'm cash-rich but time-poor. I have every intention, as the years go by, of becoming that stock comic figure: the ever-more-aged man in an ever-increasing hurry.

None of us has enough time, and we never quite make the most of it, or value it highly enough. Early on, though, I discovered a secret (a 'Secret 0', if you like). I learned that if I wanted to get more done, and make each day matter, I needed a proper structure around me. So I built one. One of the first appointments I made at HomeServe was to hire someone to manage my diary, shield me from distractions and help me focus on important tasks. I'm amazed how many leading entrepreneurs boast about doing their own admin. *Don't!* A great EA will transform your life.

These days, every day, for twenty minutes, the three pillars of my life meet: Hannah Guerin, my management assistant Ryan Hoffmann, and Jayne Neal, who after twenty-three years as my PA is most definitely one of the family whether she likes it or not. They plan my day, take some meetings, summarise and prioritise documents, sort through emails and screen replies. So I don't just 'start work'; I begin a day that's been rigorously scheduled by my support team. They make me more productive, and whatever success I've enjoyed is down to them.

When I started out, I'd measure the day by how busy I'd been. Now, slumped on the sofa, it's about how productive and efficient it's been. I set aside a couple of hours on Sunday evening to plan the week ahead and reflect on the previous one. My worst days are when I haven't found time for forty-five minutes' exercise, whether swimming, running, weights or squash. When we were married, Kate set boundaries and was strict about having family time. She and Jayne fixed things so I saw far more of my children as they grew up than I had any right to expect, given my schedule. I'm not a big person for business lunches or dinners, and I'm not comfortable with small talk. If you try to have a conversation about what we've had to eat, I'll probably just smile and mumble. Ask me about the business instead. You'll see a different person.

I tell people all the time – Jayne most of all – that I'd like to free up some time. Jayne just laughs at me: 'You're never happier than with back-to-back meetings!' I'm not sure that's true. But I do keep a notebook by the bed to scribble down ideas in the middle of the night.

You might be asking, 'How can Harpin be non-conformist if he's always following rules?' The answer is: because they're my rules. There are a lot of rules in life. Some are dumb. Some are onerous. Some will save your life. People can choose to ignore all the rules, and they will lead lives that are chaotic, frustrated and, most likely, short. Or they can choose to obey all the rules, and let life carry them along at its own speed and direction. That won't be a bad life, all in all.

But the people who create their own template and follow it – they're the ones who live up to their best life. That's the kind of success I want.

PERSISTENCE

I don't like breaking things. I'm conservative. I almost never throw out an idea, though heaven knows, I try. At night it creeps back into the house and has me think about it at odd hours, still going at it in the belief that in the end something will give and the motor will turn.

One thought I often chew over is, 'What would have become of Jeremy Middleton and me had we failed to find the way to make HomeServe work?' I like to think that, if our every entrepreneurial dream had been snatched from us, Jeremy would have ended up in some ridiculously senior role at Deloitte or PwC. He has the smarts for it. I'm not so sure about me. Look at all those companies I acquired for HomeServe, all those projects I started; I think sometimes persistence makes me stupid.

Without persistence, though, where are you? You'll fall in the first strong wind. As I said earlier, no entrepreneur is born with a perfect balance of character traits. Everyone has strengths and weaknesses. My greatest strength is persistence, and I've used persistence to make up for my failings elsewhere. Persistence has shaped my life and inevitably, because I am a leader, it's shaped others' lives as well. My idea of a good day was, and still is, a strategy day with the team that starts at 6.30 a.m. with a personal trainer and ends in the bar with everyone still relentlessly focused until the early hours on what they want to accomplish in the annual strategy meeting the day after. Some people thrive on that level of relentlessness, and those are the people who've stayed with me for well over a decade, or have left and later returned because life outside of the churn has proved duller than they can bear.

One of these people is Stella David, who was a non-exec on the HomeServe main board for ten years. When I showed her an early version of this book, however, far from singing the praises of our unceasing industry, she told me I had not given enough thought to the price others had paid to make it possible. 'What about the people who left after a year? What about all your arguments with the board?'

This drew me up. 'What arguments?'

'What about India? What about Brazil?'

These were adventures in expansion so wrong-headed they never really got started. 'I didn't see much point in describing them,' I said.

The more Stella talked, though, the more I realised I had unconsciously smoothed over some difficult material.

I'm proud of HomeServe's record of service to its people. It's not for nothing, I believe, that in 2016, Glassdoor named HomeServe UK one of its top three 'Best Places to Work'. In HomeServe's UK operation alone, 132 people have worked in the business for over twenty years, and when the business was sold, 1,445 people across the UK and our international businesses benefited from our employee share plan: this £10 million payout handed an average of £7,000 to every employee.

In my unstinting pursuit of success, however, I have led plenty of colleagues down blind alleys. And when things went right? Well, the price I expected others to pay for their success was high. You made that work? Good. Now make it work faster. You triumphed today? That's nice. What are you going to do for us tomorrow?

I've always had a fine horror of lording it over people. It's not in me to be like that. I've always celebrated others' successes and given them full credit. At the same time, according to Stella, I've never given people the time to catch their breath. For some, that's exhilarating. For others, I realise now, it's been disheartening. I'm sorry for that, and I'm certainly not going to defend it.

I learned to limit the damage. I never used my relentlessness as some sort of moral cudgel: I've been very careful never to hold a grudge, and I've tried to get better, over the years, at hiring and firing in a speedy, clear-eyed and forthright way that serves the businesses best and leaves everyone with their dignity intact. I'm certainly not going to belittle those who need a short rest after a success. Experience tells me that this describes most people! But it doesn't describe me, and it doesn't describe my businesses. If people learned that to their cost, and suffered, that's not on them. That's on me. The same applies to my private life. Did my relentlessness serve my family well? I hope to God the positives outweighed the negatives.

So here's what I've learned: you're almost certainly stronger, stranger, fiercer and more unbalanced than you think you are. Keep an eye on that greatest strength of yours. It can do real damage to the people closest to you.

*   *   *

For one of the ultimate tales of persistence, I promised to tell you the story of Craig Waddington, the man who made a fortune in bathrooms, had it taken from under him and put everything back together again – his life and his business – better than before. It speaks to a kind of persistence I think is rare these days, and becoming rarer.

Craig and his twin and their two older brothers lived in a small council house with their parents in Huddersfield. The boys had to double up, and as soon as they were old enough, the older two moved out. Craig credits his eldest brother Darren, who later became his warehouse manager, with giving him his work ethic. 'At nine, he had a paper round, and when I got to be nine, and he left home, I took it over. This gave me two paper rounds, one for the shop at the top of the hill in Cowlersley, and one for the shop at the bottom.' Glen, Craig's twin, had a milk round. 'And we had a plot of land where we kept sixty chickens and rabbits, and we'd sell them at the market on Saturdays. We must have had about sixty rabbits in the backyard at one point. When we were a bit older, I remember we'd jump in and out of skips, "wiring" as we called it, stripping the plastic off the copper and selling it – anything to make a few quid.'

At thirteen Craig started stacking shelves in the local fruit-and-veg shop. He left school with no qualifications; he was more than happy to keep working at the shop. It was no dead-end option: the owner had two stores by this point and at seventeen Craig was running one of them. Craig had a very happy childhood, he's very clear on this point – 'We were happy, and safe, and felt free' – but he came away from it with a cast-iron work ethic, an understanding that you don't get anything in life for free.

Glen had graduated from his milk round to delivering for a bathroom distribution company. 'It was Glen who drew me into the business. He figured he could run his own bathroom shop on Saturdays and Sundays by buying everything from his boss, and work as an employee during the week. I went and joined him.' Though they set themselves up as a retailer, Glen had worked as a wholesaler for years, and it came naturally to him to buy in bulk and sell to other suppliers as needed. 'Quite often we've have a fellow retailer calling us, saying, "We'll buy twenty units off you."' Glen's local knowledge was second to none, so the wholesale side of the business flourished exceptionally well.

Glen's unexpected death at an early age could have meant the end of the business, but Craig was 'determined to keep Glen's work alive. Everyone was wondering what would happen to the business because Glen was the frontman. They weren't so aware of me. I was Glen's helper back in the days when we were operating out of an old mill in the back of beyond, and my first job in the morning had been to shoo away the pigeons that were crapping all over our product. What people didn't realise (and why would they? This was all behind the scenes) was that I'd been doing all the buying and arranging all the deliveries.' And so Craig just kept going, doing what he was doing, and their company, his company now, Traditional Contemporary, went on growing.

British manufacturing didn't. 'One moment I was selling products made in Britain; the next, I was importing them from Italy. One of the first things I did, when Glen died, was jump on a plane to Italy. I came back with deals with Italian manufacturers to make everything to order. I had all my own range made. Then I went to China. I had a Chinese friend who was studying here, and it turned out that his family ran quite a big brassware business. I was, if not the first, then certainly the second British wholesaler in this sector to strike a Chinese deal.'

Traditional Contemporary was a solid, blossoming business right to the point where, just before the last recession, Craig decided to buy his warehouse. The building had a mortgage on it and was valued at £11 million. As Craig tells it, 'Then the recession hit and the banks came and said they needed to revalue the building. The banks didn't want it on their books and told me it was worth only seven million. That's what killed me – a £4 million debt out of nowhere. My advisers turned into administrators, and within eight months they had closed me down.'

All through the recession, Traditional Contemporary had made money. Craig didn't miss a single payment. He'd actually opened new stores to keep the revenues flowing. But Craig's advisers were giving him advice that turned out to be good for their friends or their own businesses, not good for Craig. 'I remember one bloke was setting up his own private equity company, which promptly invested in my main competitor. His best mate, another adviser-turned-administrator, sold my business and all my assets to that competitor. There's no point speculating on the conversations that went on; the bottom line is, I was exposed when the recession hit. I was a sitting duck.

'The only thing the banks couldn't take was my house,' Craig remembers, 'so I sold it myself, and with the funds I started again from scratch, or near enough. Within four weeks of closure, I had set straight back up, only this time with nothing, absolutely nothing, beyond four containers of Chinese shower cubicles out on the ocean somewhere which, once they landed in England, would be lost to the administrator. I rang my Chinese factory. "Quickly! You need to change the documents. Change them to Cubico!"' This was the name Craig had plucked out of the air for his new operation.

He found a little warehouse, the ships docked, the containers landed in the warehouse, and Craig was up and running again, trying to sell shower cubicles. 'I only had one idea, and that was to stick to my guns. The business I'd been running was healthy: why attempt to improve on a model that worked?' His first instinct was to wholesale them, but that wouldn't have worked: paying to ship one cubicle to Birmingham and the other to Dorset or wherever would have wiped him out before he started. So, he used the rest of his house money to buy whatever products he could get hold of – toilets, vanity units, all the things he knew he could sell – and he opened a little retail show-room in that warehouse. 'I'd gone straight back to the very beginning of my career: small showroom, warehouse at the back. I can't say I was happy; more weirdly content. I knew how to work seven days a week. I knew a few wholesalers who would want to work with me. I knew how to do exhibitions. Above all, I knew how to sell.

'Glen and I had built the first business slowly and steadily,' says Craig. 'This time I borrowed money. I couldn't have done it any other way, to get to where we are now. But it still niggles. With any luck one day we can pay people off and not have the worry of the bank hanging over us.' There's a pause, and then Craig says, 'Maybe that's too negative. I took on debt because I had ambitions to grow the business and accelerate things. I don't regret it. If you've got a business plan and you're confident that you can deliver, if you know your products and what you can achieve, then a little bit more funding will help you accelerate. Exposure is the problem. Establish what's the worst that could happen, and work from there.'

In 2020, Growth Partner bought a sizeable minority stake in the company. It's on track to exceed £100 million in turnover and has 142 stores nationwide. 'And we struggle to staff them! When we find good staff, we find that they don't want overtime, and they turn us down flat when we offer them six days a week.' It's enough to drive Craig crazy.

'Some of this is me getting old, but some of this very much *isn't*. When I was young it was up to me to gather metal and do paper rounds and breed rabbits and all sorts, and all this taught me self-reliance and gave me a work ethic. It's the first rule: you have to make your own opportunities. You can't wait for somebody to do it for you.'

Like it or not, there's some truth in the old adage. If you want to be wealthy, be born a millionaire. A lot of entrepreneurial businesses that succeed do so because their founders have pockets deep enough to lose and lose and lose again until, one day, they win.

I'm more interested in the majority of entrepreneurs who don't come from money, and have to put everything on the line. What happens to them? Well, quite often, exactly what you imagine would happen: they fail. But it's when you hit rock bottom and you find that you're still alive, and your family still loves you, and your friends are still talking to you, that you discover some kind of superpower. Like Craig, you become unstoppable.

RESILIENCE

Towards the end of my conversation with Craig Waddington, he said something that sent shivers down my back. 'Every generation says the next generation has it easy – and let's face it, you want them to have it easier. It's human nature to want your children to have more than you did. But I'm worried: somehow we've given the next generation more but we've made less of them.'

Once that idea lodges itself in your head, it's very hard to shake off. You start to see it everywhere. I even began to see it reflected in our work at HomeServe, through something Anna Maughan, our former company secretary, said to me: 'Regulation of the insurance sector has massively increased – but have you noticed how much more fearful customers are than they used to be? There's an ever-increasing number of online scams to think about, but I also think you can't underestimate the echo-chamber effects of the internet and social media. We're creating consumers – we're creating people – who are fearful of just about everything. And when you're frightened, naturally you look to the regulator to protect you. Now, because of all the small print we have to provide, it's difficult for us to present information to our customers in a way that's not overwhelming.'

The way Anna sees it – and I'm inclined to agree with her – this is not a feedback loop that leads anywhere good. 'We've become too "big-brothery",' she says. 'At some point you've got to say, "Look, beyond this point, you're going to have to let able people make their own informed decisions and then live by them."'

You weren't born resilient. No one is. You came into this world helpless and needy. Acquiring resilience requires personal effort. It also needs the encouragement of a society that takes pride in your ability to look after your own interests, as much as possible and for as long as possible. It seems sometimes that we've gone horribly far in the other direction – and at the worst possible time, too. It's obvious by now that artificial intelligence is going to drive another industrial revolution, only this time it'll be white-collar workers who will have their lives disrupted. This has got a lot of pundits running around like headless chickens, saying knowledge work is dead, that the middle classes are the new poor, and all the rest of it.

Let's take a breath.

First of all, a lot of 'knowledge work' isn't about knowledge, and a lot of 'white-collar jobs' are not white-collar. They're industrialised, regimented roles requiring little or no skill and offering next to no possibility for the worker's advancement. Rather than have people working at looms and lathes, we now stick people behind desks performing rote tasks that, while a sight safer than cotton manufacture, are just as wasteful of human potential.

How do I know this? Because I run call centres.

I've put the hours in to know what work in those environments is like, and we try to make those jobs as bearable as possible. Now we're using AI together with our traditional call-centre teams. We have digital automated services and a voicebot called Hana to guide you through them. When customer solutions are simple or we're inundated with calls (during extreme weather, for instance), Hana deals with thousands of claims simultaneously. Our customers always have the choice between Hana and a human, and when things are more complicated, humans take over. We record calls and monitor the data; we're constantly assessing how we can use AI to make us even more innovative. The feedback has been brilliant because customers' needs are being both fulfilled and predicted, and they're spending less time online or on the phone.

If a machine can do this work better than a person, then why would you consign a person to that role?

Well, comes the reply (and with it, I would imagine, a hardish stare), that person has to eat.

Worries about mass unemployment attend all new technologies – but did you know that whenever we introduce automation, employment increases? Look it up. History is clear on this point, though we keep ignoring its lessons.

So where are the jobs going to come from that AI will replace? Tech boosterists can be horribly glib about this – as though everyone who's been put out of a job is going to wake up tomorrow magically transformed: a high-level manager, skipping across the open-plan with an iPad and a dream. Actually, I think AI is going to be *much more disruptive* than we realise. It's going to force a wholesale change in the way we think about people, about craft and about trade. Among other things, it's going to force us all to be more resilient.

The good news is that AI will free us from being cogs in some great anonymous enterprise. No longer will we be deprived of work we can own and be proud of. (The weasel word in that grand sentence was, of course, 'we'. Progress is always uneven, and that's always hard to bear. But don't tell me progress is a mirage. My family were in cotton; my eldest relatives could tell you a tale or two.)

The bad news about AI (setting aside the outlandish-sounding but increasingly plausible idea that killer robots will take over the earth) is that this work you can own and be proud of is still work. It's going to take effort and imagination and, above all, resilience for you to make a go of it.

If you're working in a call centre today, and that's all you've managed to get going for you, then it is perfectly possible that you will be washing windows tomorrow, or cleaning ovens, or cleaning houses, or assembling and mending furniture.

So do it, would be my advice to the next generation. Do it, and if anyone tells you your job is demeaning – well, there's a wide vocabulary for you to choose from when formulating your reply.

Clean carpets. Sand floors. Lay bricks. Dig ditches. Tend gardens. Plant trees. Sign up to a Checkatrade trade school to learn. Work in hospitality or cut hair. The great thing about providing a service is that it opens up many different doors to success. It can't have escaped your notice that half the people I've talked to for this book either grabbed that opportunity for themselves, or were lucky enough to come from families who did. Not everyone is an entrepreneur, and everyone's entrepreneurial journey is different, but I'd wager more stories of business success arose from car washes than ever arose from call centres.

In the mid-2010s I helped set up the Apprenticeship Ambassadors Network to boost the numbers of high-level apprentices from 29,000 to 40,000 a year. We desperately needed them. The construction industry is crying out for new recruits to learn the skills that will be needed to hit the current government's target of building 1.5 million new homes. There are already about 50,000 unfilled vacancies, and the construction industry needs a million new tradespeople by 2035.

Numbers are only the start. I want to raise standards for people doing apprenticeships. Schools, especially, must be persuaded that pupils haven't 'failed' if they devote themselves to learning a skill. More recently, in 2021, I set up the HomeServe Foundation, a UK-registered charity that worked to promote apprenticeships and skills development with a goal of increasing the number of apprenticeships by 25,000 over three years to help build the workforce of the future.

Being an enthusiast about business, of course I want you to build a business worth a billion in your first decade. But let's face it, some of you might be reading this book out of pure curiosity. A billion-dollar business might be the very last thing you want. You would rather build a reputation as the best gardener in the village, or the best baker in town. And it may be that, in the end, the future belongs to you: an entrepreneur who's prepared to surf the new realities of a post-industrial, AI-enabled economy, by providing people with a service that they want.

But if you're going to keep a roof over your head, our society is going to have to start rewarding service properly – with respect, yes, and also with cold hard cash. And that's something it hasn't done in a very long time. There's a long road ahead, if we're to make this second industrial revolution work for the common good, and my guess is we're going to need all the resilience we can muster.

THE WELL-ROUNDED CHARACTER

Itemising virtues can take us only so far. At very least, we owe it to ourselves to pick off some vices. There's not much in my life that wakes me up in a cold sweat, but I can't ignore, forget or quite forgive myself for the times I *didn't listen.*

Entrepreneurs need experienced, wise and trusted mentors around them. Having a great board around me stopped me from making some potentially disastrous mistakes, and while I recognise this now, I haven't always been aware of the efforts others are going to to save me from myself.

I made up for my blinkered determination with honesty. When things went wrong, I said so. This let the people around me do their job and right the ship. Now and again, I meet chief executives who don't want to engage with the board, and it's almost always because, powerful as they are, they can't bear the idea of people giving them a ticking off. The thing is, though, leaders are as much responsible for the board's culture as for the culture of the company. Honesty fosters a can-do culture among the board that – as I discovered during the mis-selling crisis – can prove absolutely essential to the leader's survival. The board backed me because they felt they really knew me, warts and all.

Telling the truth is hard work, of course – especially to a board-room full of your peers and their Paddington Bear-grade Hard Stares. The temptation to spin a situation, or gild an accomplishment, is ever-present. Some people go through life trying to negotiate with reality, rather than facing up to it. It's as if they've never really grown out of the toddler stage. When very young children lie, it's almost charming. We understand that children are a lot smaller than the adults who might be angry with them, and so we tend to give them a free pass. Sadly, there are grown adults who never grew out of the habit. They're not bad people. They've just missed one of life's cardinal lessons: that telling the truth is always necessary and always hard to do. (Not lying is relatively easy. Telling the truth is an act of will; it takes some effort.)

Obviously, I'm not going to insult your intelligence by saying 'Don't lie' – you know not to do that. But I will say this: don't hedge. Don't prevaricate. Don't sugar whatever bitter pill it is you're having to deliver.

Self-importance is another bugbear of mine. Good leaders care for their people. Who wants to follow someone who wakes up every morning thinking they're better than their own workforce? The best leaders identify and draw out their followers' strengths. Their vision provides a focus for a communal effort. That way, they don't need to dictate, and they don't need to micromanage.

Many of the worst faults in business leaders spring from defensiveness. True leadership begins only as we learn how to listen, taking bad news and criticism on the chin. And, when we listen to others, we discover something quite startling: this one business of ours means different things to different people. Some colleagues are energised by profits, others by purpose; some admire the business's continuity of effort, others the speed with which it adapts to a changing market; some relish the freedom their work affords, others the ever-greater responsibilities they're taking on.

In his book *Built to Last*, Jim Collins makes much of this 'power of the AND'. As a leader, it's your job to create a culture in which people can entertain many obviously healthy perspectives on your business. A healthy business is not dogmatic. It should be able to embrace, say, discipline *and* creativity, analysis *and* decisive action. It – and you – should be able to manage ideas in the round.

In essence, embracing the power of the 'and' means bringing our businesses to full maturity, so that they contribute to the world and don't merely disrupt it.

Conclusion

By 2022 I thought HomeServe would grow faster if we were three separate businesses. 'Project Three' was launched to separate HomeServe EMEA, HomeServe North America and our Home Experts businesses, like Checkatrade in the UK and eLocal in the US.

We were just about to push the button on our plan – I remember, I was in Checkatrade's office in Portsmouth – when I got some startling news. Our share price had been drifting recently, as the stock market moved to reinvest in sectors that Covid had all but taken down, in particular the reawakening travel and hospitality industries. Now our shares had just shot up by 15 per cent! There was a rumour that Brookfield, the Canadian investor, was planning a bid for us.

Brookfield had been eyeing HomeServe for a while, analysing our reports and accounts and following our news. They said they wanted to look at us more closely: were we open to a conversation? We weren't really looking to sell the business, but given we had just geared up for a major change, it seemed churlish to reject a serious enquiry out of hand. We had been a public company for eighteen years, and now would be a good time to move to private ownership. If Brookfield offered the right price, and proved likely to be a responsible owner, we should listen.

There was some back and forth, but this was limited because of the regulations around listed companies. Brookfield couldn't do much because, in a listed environment, due diligence is restricted. The market runs on the principle that everyone should have equal information to ensure fair pricing. In this situation, you rely a lot on professional advisers. A listed company retains brokers, and J.P. Morgan had been ours for many years, along with UBS. We also hired

Goldman Sachs. Let's just say we weren't short of advice. We were also allowed to talk to our major shareholders. Over the years we'd built relationships with them, so we were able to gauge their mood with some confidence.

Brookfield undervalued us at first but raised their offer the more they learned about us. Finally, they offered £12 per share, a price we couldn't refuse on behalf of our shareholders. We supported the bid and made it public, and the sale began.

I wouldn't have felt nearly so confident had I not hit it off with two key figures at Brookfield. The first was Sikander Rashid, who it turned out had been stalking HomeServe for about three years. Enticed by the commercial possibilities in a sector that was having to rapidly decarbonise, Sikander had gone and bought a couple of smaller businesses: BOXT, a UK boiler installation business, and Thermondo, a business doing something similar in Germany. He kept going back to his global boss saying, '*Now* can I buy HomeServe?' After three years' observation, they had finally given him the green light.

Bruce Flatt, the global CEO of Brookfield, was another reassuring figure for me. Bruce had been with Brookfield for thirty years, and if you had invested one dollar with them back then it would be worth $111 today. But on that first meeting with Bruce, I wasn't looking for financial smarts. I wanted someone who listened, and took a lively interest in things he didn't know; someone who knew they didn't know everything and didn't try to dominate every conversation. By the end of that meeting, I knew we could do business. That's when I learned that, with billions on the line, your gut feelings and your feelings about corporate culture become even more important to your decision-making, not less.

The sale seemed to take for ever, mostly because, almost everywhere we worked, we were a regulated business. In the UK, the FCA had to approve the change of ownership. In the US, we needed approval from some local regulators, mainly in California and Florida. Some of the biggest US states weren't concerned and didn't require approvals, but one, where we had only a small number of customers, had stringent rules and held us up for a while.

We put the sale to a vote of the shareholders, but since we couldn't complete the deal until we had all the regulatory approvals, we ended up doing a kind of split exchange and completion, rather like when you buy a house. Then we all had to sit on our hands, waiting for the final approvals to trickle in.

So much for the 'how' of the sale. What about the 'why'?

I've mentioned how, in 2021, Brookfield had bought a business called BOXT. This boiler installer has an efficient online business model that lets it sell infrastructure ahead of any in-home visit. They've been installing 30,000 boilers a year. HomeServe has its own boiler installation business; we've been doing about 10,000 installations a year. Together, we reckon we can eventually push the total number of annual installations up to 100,000. Not my best anecdote, I think you'll agree – but those are just the foundations.

Now HomeServe is under private equity ownership it can afford to take a much longer-term view of its business. Brookfield have $1 trillion of assets under management and can use their resources in order to invest in long-term goals. Our shared goal is to own the infrastructure in the home by providing the financing for replacement heating systems. This way, we will end up owning a good part of the developed world's residential infrastructure.

I'm making this sound a bit like a Bond movie (*'Since you ask, James, our plan for world domination is . . .'*) but the bottom line is, decarbonising our economy is a pressing necessity, and well-capitalised, long-term strategic thinking is all that's preventing the world's entire decarbonisation bill from landing on our doormats tomorrow.

Replacing gas boilers with hybrid systems, heat pumps, solar panels, battery storage and EV charging units is complex and expensive. And I'm talking game-changingly expensive. For example, what's the single biggest thing householders can do to decarbonise their homes? They should replace their gas boilers with a heat pump. How much is a heat pump? Around £12,000. How much is a replacement gas boiler? About £2,500. So you can see the challenge. The householder desperately needs a financing arrangement that will spread the cost of their next heating system so that it doesn't ruin them. Lots of people are all over this issue, but getting the business model right is way more difficult than it looks from the outside.

In 2022 the UK government showed willing, offering a subsidy of £7,500 for a heat-pump installation. That's not nothing. But neither is it enough: how many households do you know, particularly in the current climate, have enough loose change to cover a £4,500 shortfall?

Our current thinking at HomeServe is to provide heat pumps and solar operating leases over fifteen years. It's a worry-free monthly payment that comes with an annual service and breakdown cover – and our profit will come from the fact that the lease generates more profit than installations alone.

Since 2015, HomeServe has been acquiring independently run businesses: local HVAC installers with good local reputations. They keep their brand name. We put in our software system, help with the marketing, and set things up so that these businesses can offer insurance policies and now operating leases, not just annual service plans. Today we've got about 150 of these local businesses across the US, France, Spain, Belgium, Germany and the UK – and thanks to our training and up-to-date systems, and the potential savings from bulk purchasing, they're providing innovative energy solutions at prices people can actually afford.

Tom Rusin, CEO of HomeServe USA, tells me that some state regulators now require that utility companies move customers to energy-efficient solutions. We reckon this puts HomeServe USA into a winning market position.

I'll always remember the worst piece of advice I ever received. With HomeServe going great guns, someone told me, 'Well, Richard, if you haven't made it by forty, you never will.' Rubbish. The best entrepreneurs are often those who've spent decades watching, learning, doing and dreaming. It's never too late.

These past few years, in my reinvention from CEO to investor, mentor and chairman, I've met many later starters. Approaching or in their middle age, with a mortgage, family and a wealth of experience, they worry that time and circumstance are against them. I tell them they should stop worrying. Then I show them my career plan for the next twenty-five years.

Most recently, and from my experiences at INSEAD, I have put together my bespoke service, Coachment, combining mentorship and business coaching. Meanwhile my investment company Growth Partner, run by Jason Mahendran, targets and helps businesses that are, at the stage we invest, making profits of between £1 million and £5 million per year. Through my purchase of *Business Leader* magazine and podcast, I'm developing a peer group membership community for founders and CEOs that will provide peer-to-peer forums, coaching and masterclasses. We'll also help you to find finance – ideally, equity investment – to help your business to grow, take on more risk and become a large company. I also spend more than a day a week supportings Shaun Prime, *Business Leader*'s CEO, helping inspire breakthrough in medium-sized businesses (those with revenues of over £3 million and more than 15 but fewer than 250 employees). There are 75,000 of these businesses in the UK, and we are helping them to grow. And so on, and so on.

We're not just living longer lives these days. We're living healthier lives. So why not make the most of them? Seriously, why retire? Are you really going to go from flat-out and full-time to a full bank account and an empty work calendar? How do you feel about that? Despite his £74 million payday, Kevin Byrne, the founder of Checkatrade, openly admits that he should never have put his feet up after selling out. There are many founder-entrepreneurs who feel as Kevin does. You need to retain a sense of purpose and fulfilment.

In 1997, Kate and I got married and moved to Lenton Road in Nottingham, right next to the old deer park and five minutes from the castle. We lived there for three years, until the birth of our first child, Jemima. By then I was travelling a lot for work, and Kate's parents, back in Yorkshire, weren't getting any younger, so in the summer of 2000 we decided to move back to Yorkshire. (I'd spent the first four or five years of my life there and I wanted my children to have roots.)

On 1 September, the front page of the *Yorkshire Post* property supplement ran a picture of The Old Vicarage in Nun Monkton. One very cold and wet and rainy Monday evening I stepped off the train from Birmingham and went to visit it. It was everything we wanted, in a nice village, with a school and a church and a pub, and it meant that Kate was only fifteen minutes away from her parents in Collingham. We decided then and there to buy. There was a lot of other interest, so I spent far too much money in a bid the vendors couldn't refuse. Seven years after moving to Nun Monkton, an even grander and more beautiful property unexpectedly became available: The Priory, Nun Monkton's magnificent main hall. I was determined to buy it and even managed to secure first refusal before it officially hit the market. But I couldn't convince Kate: 'It's too big! Aren't we happy where we are?' Despite my best efforts, she remained unconvinced – right up until the news came through that the place had been sold. It's true what they say: you don't know what you've had (or could have had) till it's gone.

I gritted my teeth and called the owner to offer my congratulations. 'We're exchanging contracts tomorrow,' he told me. 'Okay,' I blurted – who needs a brain when you've got a mouth? – 'I'll offer you a million pounds more.' But he was a man of his word: 'I can't do that,' he said. Well, you have to respect that. Half an hour later I rang him up again and offered him two million more. 'Transfer two million into my bank account this afternoon,' he told me, 'and I'll consider your offer.' My lawyer was horrified: 'You haven't had a survey, you haven't done any searches, it's madness!' Half an hour later I transferred two million pounds against my lawyer's advice.

So, we had our dream home, only to hear, a few years later, that our village pub was closing down. Since 1853, the Alice Hawthorn – named after one of Britain's greatest racehorses – has been serving the people of Nun Monkton. For a long time it was unloved and aimless, serving ready meals and an uninspiring range of drinks. When its survival came into question, and with more confidence than skill, I stepped in and bought it for £525,000. I never wanted to run a hospitality venture, but it's different when you're helping your own community.

It took me ages to find the right people to run the place. First, I got a neighbour in, lent him £50,000 and let him run it rent-free. He worked like a dervish and lost all my money. Then there was the couple who ran a restaurant in York, who discovered they couldn't be in two places at once. Then their chef, who took the place over with his daughter and had no better luck than anyone else.

It was only when I thought about what made HomeServe such a success that I found the right formula. I faced up to the brutal facts. I had to find a proven leader or leaders with skills I didn't possess, give them equity in the business and proper accountability, and set them free to make their own decisions.

I soon found a husband-and-wife team who have brilliant abilities in the kitchen (him) combined with a fabulous business brain and front-of-house skills (her). Thanks to John and Claire Topham, turnover in a good month is now about £200,000; it was £20,000 when I took over. The Tophams own half the shares in the pub, and until we turned a profit, I bankrolled the losses. (The financial benefits were less important to me than just making my village pub great.)

We didn't invent a new business. We copied what we saw would work and adapted as we went. As a family, we toured the Cotswolds to assess other pubs and hotels, and found inspiration at the Wild Rabbit, Lady Bamford's pub-with-rooms in Chipping Norton. We're all also hugely indebted to my ex-wife, Kate, who did an amazing refurbishment job on our pub, then turned a derelict barn into a private dining room and added twelve bedrooms.

In 2022, the Alice Hawthorn was, according to *The Sunday Times*, one of the hundred best places to eat out in the UK; it came top of the list in the whole of the north of England. The venture has been successful because we're always listening and learning, refining the business so that we're offering not just what we think is right but what customers say they want. Especially at this scale, word-of-mouth recommendations have proved infinitely more important than expensive marketing – a difficult lesson for me, as an ex-marketeer.

Should you find yourself visiting, book early, and don't be alarmed if you spot me dashing out of the pub and across the village green, carefully balancing trays of Estrella beer and tandoori monkfish. Though I part-own the business, I still have to book three days ahead to get a table, and if I forget I end up becoming my own home-delivery service.

If you want to take stock of your life and career, I recommend juggling hot food, at speed, across a village green. At such moments you remember that (with apologies to John Lennon) pretty much everything that matters in your life happened while you were making other plans.

It's at moments like this that you will know whether or not you are happy. Happiness can't be pursued, the way we can pursue our billion. Happiness arises along the way. I pursued success in business because I loved business. You may be reading this just for fun, and your idea of success may look very different to mine. Good on you. We will still meet at the end, wondering what on earth happened to us while we were making other plans.

What did we take from people, and what did we give? What are we leaving behind, and does it matter? What did we learn?

It took me nine steps to get where I am now (hungry, hands full, stumbling over cowpats, covered in some sort of sauce). I've couched these steps as business lessons in this book, because I know about business and I know that these lessons will be of some practical value to you. But it doesn't take much effort to see that, behind the details, there lie some handy guides to life in general:

- Accept how the world is and learn everything you can about it, in pursuit of what you want.
- Figure out what road you're taking and look for company on that road.
- The lessons you pass on (whether you meant to or not) will outlast your grandest monuments, so create your best legacy: learn how to teach.
- Embrace all the opportunities of your time; new ideas are scary, and old ideas are dull, only because you make them so.

- Make things for the joy of making them, and hand them on.
- Relish people's variety and respect it.
- Try looking at the world through one window; you'll see more.
- Try to be better.

I've often said to my children that what matters is not how you play the game; it's whether you win. Obviously, I'm having a bit of fun. But this isn't just wordplay. We all know decent people who have lost at life, one way or another. We all know dreadful people who seem to sail through life without a worry. And there are decent people who do make good lives for themselves, and many scoundrels who do come undone. Life's good, but no one said it was fair or made much sense.

Since you don't have to choose between winning and being a decent human being, why not do both? Why else did the world put you here? To mark time? To suck up air? It's not enough to play the game well. You owe it to the world to try to win it.

I do a lot of sport, choosing activities I enjoy and some that I force myself into even though I don't enjoy them as much. I'm lucky enough to have a squash court in Yorkshire, so I try to play squash regularly. But I'm realistic. I know there will come a day when my knees won't be up to squash any more. When that happens, I'll switch to padel. I'm planning to build a padel court in my village, Nun Monkton, for myself, the pub regulars, the school kids – everyone, really. I never really enjoyed running, so I didn't do a proper half marathon until I was fifty-nine, had just got off a twelve-hour flight and hadn't eaten for two and a half days (food poisoning). I just couldn't let my sons down, and anyway, I wanted to beat them. This did not happen.

In Japan there's a principle called *ikigai* – 'a reason for being'. It will help you be more successful. But there's more: the clearer your direction, the more you will be able to help and inspire people along the way.

I went on a holiday to Rhodes recently, and when I got back to the house in Marylebone, Jayne Neal, my PA, was there to greet me. 'Did you have fun?' she asked me.

'Yeah,' I said. 'Great! Cycling every single morning! Up at seven! Forty-five to sixty kilometres, and back for lunch . . . What?' I couldn't for the life of me see what was so funny. Scowling, I went into the kitchen to read some transcripts.

While I'd been away, a researcher had interviewed Jayne:

'Richard is more curious now. He's looking for opportunities in different areas of business. He was pretty single-minded when he set up HomeServe. He's having more fun these days. You can see the pleasure he radiates when he finds he can help someone with their business.

'There are financial criteria for what he's doing at Growth Partner, but it's the people running this or that company who pique his interest first. I know this because he's always waving newspaper cuttings in the air: "Right, Jayne, get me a meeting with them!"'

Workbook

'To will implies delay, therefore now do.'
– John Donne

Begin your nine-step journey by answering these questions. Take your time and write down your answers. Writing is thinking, so use whole sentences. Create a statement that you can look back on in future.

1. Copy and Pivot
   - What gap in the market are you filling?
   - What are you copying? What are you improving?
   - What is it about you and your business that will encourage investors to back you?
   - Have you now got a business model that is working?

2. Find an Investor
   - What's the least amount of money you'd need to take your mind off day-to-day worries and focus exclusively on your business? Think, first, to repay a mortgage or friends and family. Then look for cash to grow, e.g., to increase the size and quality of your management team.
   - What kinds of questions would you have to ask to know whether a potential investor shared your sense of purpose?
   - What kinds of network, skills and contacts do you expect to get from your chosen investor?

3. Get Some Coachment
   - What's your biggest challenge or opportunity right now that a coach could help you with?
   - What specific business knowledge or experience are you looking for in a mentor?
   - Who would be your ideal mentor, and your ideal coach? What are you going to do, today, to get in touch with them and ask for their help?

4. Bricks and Clicks and Paper
   - Does your business operate across all channels? Are you making the most of the opportunities of bricks, clicks and paper?
   - What's your weakest channel? Why? And what, today, can you do about that?
   - Is there a missing channel that you should be working on?
   - How integrated are your business channels? Where are they working well together? Where are they stealing from each other?
   - If applicable, do you have any strategic retail partners? Which (other) major stores would you like to talk to? Who should you call?

5. Hire Your Replacement
   - Are you ready to hire your replacement? What's holding you back?
   - What sort of person needs to replace you, and how are you going to go about recruiting them?
   - Soon (unless you retire – which I don't recommend) you will be looking for your new role in the business. Where do your real strengths lie?
   - What other key roles are missing from your organisation today?

6. Go Global with Locals
   - Is there an opportunity to expand your business internationally?
   - Is now the right time, or not?
   - Which is the right new country to focus on, and why?
   - Are you ready to spend time in that country to really understand it?
   - Are you ready to hire local country managers? Where will you find them and how will you recruit them?
   - Are you clear what local suppliers you will need? Are you already in touch with them? How will you foster these relationships?

7. Evolution, Not Revolution
   - What is your next evolution? Are you sure it is not a revolution?
   - How are you going to keep evolving?
   - Do you have more evolutionary ideas to test and prove out?

8. Follow a *Not*-to-do List
   - Do you have a hedgehog strategy? If not, shouldn't you work with your team on putting one together?
   - How will you make sure everyone in your business knows what it is and only works on those priorities that fit the strategy?
   - Are you confident that you still have a very simple and clear business model?

9. Hone Your Character
   - Write down up to six words that describe your character strengths.
   - What are your weaknesses or development areas?
   - What are the parts of your job today that you don't enjoy?
   - Do you have three behaviours or values that guide you?
   - Will you be doing the same role or a different one in five years' time?
   - Do you have a ten-year career plan?

What Next?

I hope these nine steps have resonated with you and that you can apply more than one or two to your business. If this book has helped you to think bigger, my company, Business Leader, could give you the structure, support and community to turn insight into action.

It's a private network for founders and CEOs running businesses with revenue of over £3 million and more than fifteen employees. If you're ready to scale with pace, precision and peer support, this is your next move.

Workshops

If you're an ambitious entrepreneur turning over around £3 million in revenue, why not come along to one of my free weekly Business Leader Growth Workshops at my home in London?

These are relaxed, small-group sessions (just twelve founders and CEOs) where I share practical growth lessons from the book, and we discuss how these work in practice, together. They offer a great chance to dive into the learning in person.

Scan the QR code below to book your spot.

Stage-based peer group forums
Be matched with ten ambitious founders and CEOs at your growth stage. Led by a professional coach, these confidential sessions are where real challenges are solved, bold ideas are tested and momentum is built.

Nine Steps coaching framework
Bring the ideas in this book to life through structured, stage-specific one-to-one coaching, designed to help you grow your revenue from £3 million to £100 million and beyond.

World-class content and masterclasses
Access exclusive insight through weekly live events, expert-led masterclasses, *Business Leader* magazine, award-winning podcasts and premium newsletters.

Company visits, awards and events
Go behind the scenes at Britain's most impressive businesses, attend curated dinners and celebrate success at our Growth 500 and six-monthly summits.

A network that moves you forward
Surround yourself with other ambitious and successful founders and CEOs who think big, act decisively and believe in raising the bar – together.

Learn more about us at www.businessleader.co.uk/membership.

Acknowledgements

It turns out that the writing of a book is not that different to growing a business. It involves a great team, all coming together to make something out of a shared vision – and the Nine Steps can be followed pretty well, too!

And so I have some thanks to those who've helped me follow my Nine Steps when it came to *How to Make a Billion in Nine Steps*.

Copy and Pivot: My agent, Max Edwards at Apple Tree Literary, saw the potential in the Nine Steps, and how we could copy from some of the great business books and pivot to make the fresh approach that you've just read. My thanks, too, to Alex Osmond and Tom Lloyd-Williams in his team.

Find an Investor: The team at Piatkus have been brilliant throughout. Tom Asker originally acquired the book and Elena Roberts took over the editorial mantle in seeing it through to publication when Tom left for pastures new. The book wouldn't be half as good without their fantastic notes and would not have seen bookshelves without their investment.

Get some Coachment: Simon Ings worked incredibly closely with me throughout the process, helping me to find the words to write *How to Make a Billion in Nine Steps*. A wonderfully experienced writer, I couldn't have asked for a better person to work with me throughout the writing of this book.

Brick and Clicks and Paper: Narjas Zatat at Piatkus, Savannah Fischl and Ryan Hoffmann in my team, and Lisa Jarrett-Kerr at Teneo were crucial at getting the word out. If you found out about this book through the media or online, it was probably because of them.

Hire Your Replacement: If I were to pack this whole book thing in tomorrow, I'd know that my brilliant COO, Hannah Guerin, would be able to step into the reins immediately. She's been with me every step of the way and her insight, good humour and incredible hard work, make everything tick. Thank you.

Go Global with Locals: My thanks to those at Piatkus who helped make this work in multiple territories: to John Fairweather for managing the book's production, to Amanda Keats as the managing editor, and to Caitriona Row and Barbara Ronan for overseeing sales.

Evolution, Not Revolution: What you've read here doesn't change anyone's view of business – instead, I hope, it's an evolution of things you'll already know. Everyone at HomeServe – past and present – and everyone else throughout my business career has helped me realise that. My particular thanks in helping me to evolve into the next stage of my career must go to the close team around me – in particular, to Jayne Neal. I couldn't do it without you.

Follow a Not-to-do-List: One of the most crucial parts of any book is its cover. We went round and round on it, until we realised what we *didn't* want from it – and so my thanks to Meg Shepherd for her great design.

Hone Your Character: The most important people to thank are of course those who know me best and have made me who I am today. To my mother, and brother, Stephen, who supported my early entrepreneurial businesses, and Jeremy Middleton, my co-founder and business partner. I couldn't have done it without you. To my ex-wife Kate for her support and most importantly to Jemima, Tom and Woozy.

And finally, a big thank you to everyone I have mentioned in this book who has helped me on my entrepreneurial journey – and to all those I haven't mentioned. Special thanks go to Brian Whitty, Barry Gibson, Tommy Breen, Stella David, Katrina Machin, Ron McMillan, Anna Maughan, Emma Thomas, Julian Woolley, Ed Bolas, Linda Hardy, Chris Day, Alanna Barron, David White, Kate Grocott-Mason, James Hamilton and Andrew Osipov.

Index

About the author

Richard Harpin is famous for breeding rabbits (and pulling them out of hats; he had a brief career as a stage magician), grading and bagging conkers, marketing fishing flies as earrings, and building a home repairs and services company worth over £4 billion. He was born in Huddersfield in 1964, lost tens of thousands of pounds a year expanding the wrong business model, found the right one, and spent most of the rest of his life flying himself from one international outpost to another in planes and helicopters. He has just finished writing his business plan for the next twenty-five years.

Richard reckons there are nine steps to building a billion-pound business, and he could have got there a lot sooner had he known what they were before he started. Now he's out to save the next generation from his mistakes: he writes a business column for *The Sunday Times*, steers a leadership organisation and backs other entrepreneurs with his own money.